HOW TO LIVE
ICELANDIC

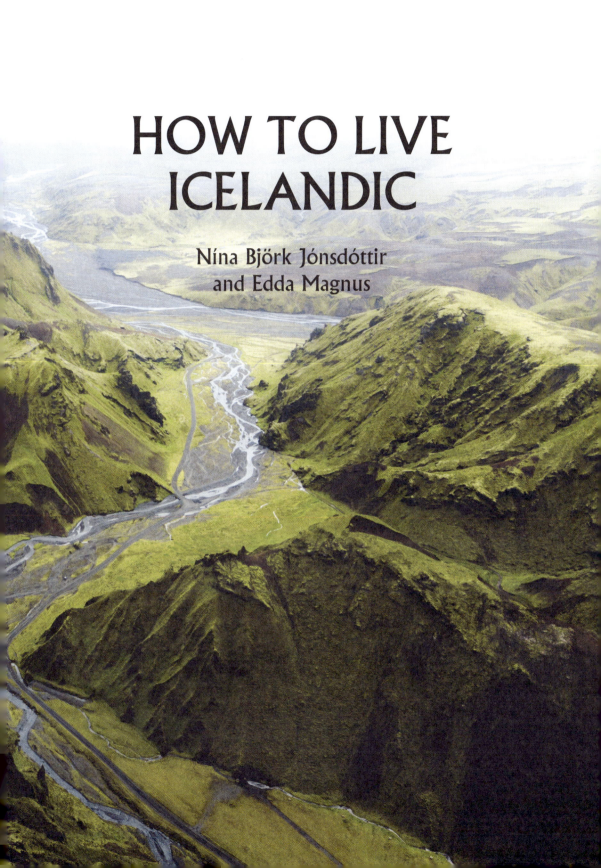

HOW TO LIVE ICELANDIC

Nína Björk Jónsdóttir
and Edda Magnus

INTRODUCTION	06
AREAS OF ICELAND	08
WHAT MAKES THE ICELANDERS	44
CULTURE	68
AT THE TABLE	96
LIFE OUTDOORS	120
LIFE INSIDE	144
FAMILY LIFE AND LIFE'S MILESTONES	164
HOLIDAYS AND CELEBRATIONS	188
PICTURE CREDITS	222
ABOUT THE AUTHORS	223

Introduction

How can one describe what it means to call somewhere home?

The feeling of lying on a soft bed of sun-baked moss covering an ancient lava field.

The sweet smell of a birch forest just after the rain.

The salty wind, so strong it takes your breath away, that never fails to welcome you home when you step out of Keflavík Airport.

The waves of goosebumps over your body as you step into the warm hot tub after the run from the showers to the outdoor pool.

The buzzing energy of a bright summer's night when you stumble out of a nightclub at 3 a.m.

The stillness of a frozen winter's night when the only sound is the snow crackling under your feet as the northern lights dance in the sky above you.

The warm feeling of belonging when the clock strikes midnight on New Year's Eve and everyone in your street, your town and your country joins you in the celebration.

The overwhelming sense of relief and gratitude when the local farmer skips dinner to come outside and tow your car out of a ditch during a snowstorm.

In this book, we attempt to bring Iceland, the place we call home, to life with all its sensations. Journeying through breathtaking landscapes, tiny coastal villages and the bustle of Reykjavík, we will explore Iceland's favourite foods, pastimes and the major milestones and festivities in our lives. We will celebrate our athletes, artists, writers and musicians, as well as Iceland's role as a world leader in sustainability, renewable energy and gender equality.

The incredible and unpredictable nature at our doorstep; the freedom of an Icelandic childhood; belonging to a close-knit society where every individual can thrive; our ability to not take ourselves too seriously; and our stoically optimistic approach to life, which has helped us survive centuries of poverty, bad weather and natural disasters: these are the unique qualities that make us who we are. This is how to live Icelandic.

AREAS OF ICELAND

Land of Fire and Ice

In geological terms, Iceland is very young: a country still in the making. The earth is about 4.5 billion years old, but the oldest rock in Iceland is only around 16 million years old. The country sits on the Mid-Atlantic Ridge, where the Eurasian and North American tectonic plates are slowly drifting apart, tearing Iceland in opposite directions to the west and east by around 2 centimetres (0.8 inches) a year. The juncture lies through the middle of the country, where volcanic activity is concentrated, making the western and easternmost parts of Iceland the oldest.

In many ways, Iceland is a living textbook on geology. If you look out of the airplane window when approaching Keflavík Airport, you can see cracks in the lava field below all running in the same direction. It looks a bit like a cake that has been left for too long in the oven. The landscape at Þingvellir National Park is testament to this, with its ravines and rock walls all lined in the same direction. The plates on the ocean floor stretch in opposite directions, causing tension to build up in the earth's crust that is released through earthquakes and volcanic eruptions, forming the Mid-Atlantic Ridge. Beneath Iceland is an additional mantle plume with even more volcanism, causing the island to rise out of the ocean – hence 'land of fire'.

As the name suggests, Iceland is also a country of ice (although not as much as nearby Greenland, despite their names!). Its high latitude, just below the Arctic Circle (although the Circle does go through Grímsey island), accounts for roughly 10 per cent of Iceland being covered with glaciers. Some of Iceland's most active volcanoes, such as Grímsvötn and Katla, are located under glaciers.

AREAS OF ICELAND

There are some common misconceptions about Iceland. Firstly, it is not as cold as you might think. We have the Gulf Stream to thank for that – the ocean current that brings warm water from the Gulf of Mexico into the Atlantic Ocean, making the climate in Iceland much warmer in winter than it would otherwise be. Winters in Iceland tend to be mild, while the summers are cool. The average temperature in Reykjavík is about 0°C (32°F) in the coldest months and 11°C (52°F) at the peak of summer. It might sound like we have the same climate all year, but as an old Icelandic joke goes, if you don't like the weather, just wait for five minutes. On any given day, you could have rain, wind, snow, hail and sun thrown at you within a very short time. The forecast has to be quite good for Icelanders to consider leaving the house without a coat.

Another misconception is that Iceland is small. In actual fact, it covers 103,000 square kilometres (40,000 square miles), so it's larger than many European countries, including Hungary, Austria and Portugal (each, not combined). This allows quite a lot of space for around 370,000 inhabitants, making Iceland the least densely populated country in Europe.

The Sea Gives, the Sea Takes

Almost all Icelanders live on the coast, of which about two-thirds are located in and around the capital, Reykjavík. The rest of the population lives in towns and villages or on farms. Most towns tend to be rather small (between 500–5,000 inhabitants is common) and they are often close to natural harbours.

Most Icelanders are used to seeing the ocean every day. However, our attitude towards it is perhaps different to other island nations. We see the water more as a workplace and source of food and revenue than a place for leisure. We are very conscious of the fact that the north Atlantic is dangerous. Seafaring was, until quite recently, a perilous undertaking. Most Icelanders have grown up with both fear and respect for the sea, an ambivalence summed up in the old saying, '*Hafið gefur, hafið tekur*' – 'the sea gives, the sea takes'.

However, our relationship with the sea is changing, not least due to increased safety. With improved technology, training, better equipment and protective gear, fishing has now become as safe as any other industry. Icelanders have also started to use the ocean for recreation, although our heated swimming pools hold more appeal. That said, some people have taken up sea bathing, even in winter, as many believe dipping your body into cold water is good for your health. It certainly feels exhilarating. An artificial 'geothermal beach' has been created in Nauthólsvík in Reykjavík, where you can go straight into the hot tub or take a hot shower after bathing in the sea.

Vestmannaeyjar – Pompeii of the North

There are very few natural harbours along the south coast of Iceland. In fact, the only natural harbour on the 400-kilometre (249-mile) stretch between Þorlákshöfn in the west and Höfn in the east (*höfn* means 'harbour') is in the Vestmannaeyjar archipelago, making the islands an important centre for fishing.

On 23 January 1973, an eruption began on Heimaey, the main island, close to the centre of a town of almost 5,300 people. Never before in the history of Iceland had an eruption started so close to a residential area. Luckily, the weather had been poor the day before, so most of the local fishing boats were in harbour and could be used to evacuate all the inhabitants to the mainland in the middle of the night. That harbour, the lifeline of the town, was threatened by the flow of the lava, but scientists came up with the idea of pumping seawater straight onto the lava to make it solidify, thereby changing the course of its flow. The eruption lasted until 3 July that year, covering the town in ash and burying houses under lava. About two-thirds of the inhabitants moved back after the eruption and the town was soon thriving again.

One of the homes ruined by the eruption has been dug out and forms part of Eldheimar, a museum where you can learn about the eruption and visit the excavated house which, a bit like Pompeii, is almost frozen in time, with coffee cups on the table and children's toys on the floor. Today, Eldfell (Iceland's youngest mountain) rises above the town and it's only a short hike to the top. Half a century later, a lot of heat remains – if you dig into the gravel you can feel it. Locals bring tins or milk cartons filled with ryebread dough, bury it in the warm gravel and come back 24 hours later to collect their volcano-baked loaves.

'Life is Salted Cod'

'Life is salted cod' is a philosophy found in Halldór Laxness's epic novel *Salka Valka*, about an everyday heroine of the same name. It sums up a well-known truth in Iceland: life is fish and fish is life.

The waters around Iceland are among the best fishing grounds in the world and contain a great variety of species. The Gulf Stream meeting the ice-cold sea coming down from the Arctic creates excellent conditions for rich marine life.

Icelanders have been fishing since the first settlement, mainly for their own subsistence. Dried cod was exported abroad from the fourteenth century. In the nineteenth century, salt became available, making it possible to create a more valuable export. Fishing was done on open boats and conditions were often very dangerous, as the main fishing season was usually in winter when workers, otherwise occupied on farms, were available to man the boats and process the fish.

Other nations started fishing in Icelandic waters from the fifteenth century. First came the English, then the Germans, the Basques, the Dutch and the French. Pierre Loti's novel *Pêcheur d'Islande* (*An Iceland Fisherman*) explains the conditions on board and the lives of the men from Brittany and French Flanders who spent a good part of the year in the perilous waters around Iceland. The French first started to fish around Iceland in the seventeenth century and the last French fishermen were seen in 1938. Their peak was from around 1860 until the First World War. It is estimated that around 400 *goélettes* (schooners) were lost at sea and more than 4,000 French fishermen drowned. The first hospitals in Iceland were actually built by the French government to tend to sick fishermen – a clear indication of the size and importance of fishing in Icelandic waters for France's economy. You can visit the old French hospital and an excellent museum about the history of the fishermen in the town of Fáskrúðsfjörður, where the 'French days' festival is celebrated every year (see page 220).

AREAS OF ICELAND

Foreign nations fishing in Iceland's waters came to an end in the so-called 'Cod Wars' with the United Kingdom over three periods between 1958 and 1976. Iceland extended its territorial waters unilaterally and the UK disapproved, sending Royal Navy vessels to protect British trawlers that continued to fish within the limit. The Icelandic Coast Guard developed a method to cut fishing nets from trawlers. The dispute ended when the UK conceded to a 200-nautical miles limit.

Fishing remains the mainstay of the Icelandic economy, although it has greatly diversified in recent decades. It is an important source of food and is, unsurprisingly, deeply connected to the identity of Icelanders.

Sustainability and the Sea

For a country so dependent on the sea, preservation of the marine environment is vital. In 1980, Iceland introduced a fish-management system to ensure sustainable fisheries and protect living marine resources for future generations. The total allowable catch is decided annually for each species, based on scientific advice. The management system is coupled with effective enforcement and control. For instance, if a high number of juvenile fish is found in a particular fishing ground, the area can be closed down quickly without warning.

In recent years, sustainability in the fishing industry has been taken to the next level through innovation and research. Icelandic fishing companies are at the forefront of sea technology, developing environmentally friendly and sustainable solutions for the whole value chain, from designing and building better fishing vessels to resources and reducing waste. Iceland is now a big exporter of innovative solutions that increase the value of seafood caught, reduce waste and safeguard the environment. Automation in fish processing has transformed fish factories and made it possible to maximise yield, making sure nothing goes to waste. Another breakthrough is that parts of the fish previously thrown away, such as skin and bones, are now being used to create a variety of valuable products, from skin treatments for chronic wounds to food supplements and cosmetics.

Community and the Coast

You might drive through a small Icelandic coastal town and wonder if anything much ever happens there. All you see is a few houses, a fish factory, the harbour, the school, the church, the old people's home and a petrol station. However, there is much more to life on the coast than first meets the eye.

Maður er manns gaman ('Man is Man's Joy') is an old saying from *Hávamál*, one of the books of the *Poetic Edda*. Small towns tend to have a rich cultural life. Most municipalities have an ambitious music school with professional teachers, a church choir (and perhaps more choirs, see page 158) and an amateur theatre group (see page 159). They organise the best Þorrablót parties (see page 207). There will also be a rescue team (see page 126), and formal groups where people work together for their community and raise money for charities. In particular, there has been a strong tradition of *kvenfélög* (women's associations) since the 1870s.

Today, the demographic of these coastal villages often varies to other parts of the country, with a higher proportion of people of overseas origin who have found work in the fishing industry. Many villages host Þjóðahátíð festivals, where those who have settled from abroad introduce villagers to their own cultures and traditions.

Every Icelander knows that nature can be dangerous. This fact is perhaps nowhere as present as in coastal villages. Many villages are located in fjords at the bottom of steep mountains, where the risk of avalanches is very real during the winter months. Structural avalanche protection has been built to protect most of them and the risk is monitored day and night. Fortunately, avalanches close to homes are very rare, but people who live in high-risk areas are used to having to evacuate until it is safe to return.

Growing up in a fishing town gives kids unparalleled access to nature. They play in the harbour, hike in the mountains to pick berries in summer and ski in the winter. People sometimes go out to sea for recreational sea angling. The water can be very calm in narrow fjords and going out on a kayak at midnight at the peak of summer is magical.

Farmers at Heart

Icelanders are the descendants of farmers – indeed, the sagas have jokingly been summarised as 'farmers fought each other'. The Vikings brought livestock such as sheep, cows and horses with them (the arctic fox was the only mammal in Iceland at the time of settlement) and for centuries, farming was the main economic activity in Iceland. As an example of the great esteem given to the profession, co-author Nína's great-grandfather Þórður Sveinsson, Iceland's first psychiatrist, was sent away to pursue his studies on the basis that his health was weak and it was thought that he would never make a good farmer.

Over the centuries, the pursuit of agriculture has been no mean feat. Conditions are limited due to the cool climate, the short growing season and a lack of suitable land. It is not surprising that agriculture has declined relative to the rest of the economy, and today it only accounts for less than two per cent of the workforce. There are about 3,000 farms and these are mostly small family holdings. The bulk of production is milk and lamb, as well as some poultry and pig farms, and greenhouse-based horticulture. Almost no corn is grown in Iceland, though. Farming is highly subsidised and farmers often struggle to make ends meet, which is why many offer accommodation for tourists, rent out horses or allow people to build summer houses on their land. Farmers often have seasonal workers to help out, often young people from abroad who come to stay in Iceland for a few weeks.

Despite the declining economic importance of agriculture, Icelanders are still farmers at heart. Urbanisation is a relatively new phenomenon, so every Icelander can trace their roots to farms around the country and many older people almost certainly spent summers in their youth helping out on a farm. Agriculture continues to be held in high regard, both for cultural reasons and to maintain a rural population, as well as to ensure local food production – of particular importance for a nation dependent on all imported goods being transported over long distances by air or sea.

Life on the farm is greatly affected by the seasons. Lambing season in May is the busiest time of the year. In early summer, sheep are taken up to the mountains, where they will stay until September. When driving in the countryside and on Highland roads, you'll often come across ewes with their young, so it's important to drive carefully, as the lambs will likely run across the road if their mother is on the other side.

For centuries, milk was the only fresh product that was supplied throughout the year, so it was very important to have a good milking cow. Due to the climate, cows and other animals are kept inside for longer than in most countries, so it is quite a spectacle when they are let out in spring.

As the weather is notoriously changeable, Icelanders are known for working very hard when conditions are favourable, for instance, collecting the hay when the grass is dry. In summer, when there is sunlight through the night, you might even see people working the fields into the small hours.

A major event in the autumn is the *réttir*, when local farmers work together to bring their sheep down from the mountains where they have spent the summer roaming free. They are herded into enclosures with smaller pens on

AREAS OF ICELAND

the outside. The farmers then go into the crowd of sheep, looking for the markings of their farm, then drag their sheep into their pen on the outside. The *réttir* is a fun occasion, a celebration of tradition. People pass a bottle around, sing songs and enjoy themselves.

There are other events related to sheep farming in some areas, such as the 'beauty contest' of the *forystufé* (leader sheep), where the most beautiful ram of this specific breed, only found in Iceland, is selected based on his behaviour, colouring, leg length and other aspects. As their name suggests, leader sheep lead the flock when they are being moved to the mountains and back down again. They are known for being extra-sturdy and good at finding their way, even in bad weather.

Horticulture is an important farming activity. Greenhouses are found in areas close to geothermal hotspots – some farmers cultivate flowers, such as roses; others tomatoes, cucumbers, peppers, herbs and fruit; and there are those that grow outdoor plants to sell. Friðheimar is a family-run farm at Reykholt in the heart of the agricultural south, where you can see tomato production, taste the harvest and buy products such as jam, salsa and juice. There is also a restaurant serving tomato-based dishes.

A very important feature of life in the countryside is to always have coffee, and something to have with it, such as *kleinur* – delicious twisted doughnuts. Having a big freezer is also vital and farmers go into towns to bulk-buy, as many Icelandic farms are quite remote.

Children are largely left to their own devices, often helping around the farm. They are collected each morning by the school bus and brought home in the evening. Most children live no more than 30 minutes from school, but in remote areas some will travel an hour each way, on often treacherous roads.

There is also a strong sense of community in rural areas. People help each other and everybody knows everybody (as did their ancestors). As in coastal towns and villages, there is a wide range of community activities. There are also 450 *ungmennafélög* – youth clubs based on a more than a century of tradition. These clubs organise social activities for young people such as sports, forestry and nature protection, as well as learning about democracy, equality and peace, with the aim of building strong individuals that will contribute to society.

The Highlands – Feeling the Smallness of Man

To fully understand the intense beauty of Iceland, you must visit the Icelandic Highlands. This area, known as *Hálendið*, covers more than a third of the country and represents one of the largest areas in Europe that has never been inhabited and where humans have left very little impact.

The Highlands are a breathtaking wilderness of glaciers, volcanoes, lava fields and black sand. The landscape is truly surreal. With no trees blocking your view, you can feel like you are the only person on earth. It is in moments like this that you realise the smallness of man against the monumental forces of nature.

The only people to have lived in the Highlands were *útilegumenn* – outlaws (literally 'men who lie outside'). Such people were condemned or accused of crimes and took to the Highlands to escape justice. Somehow, they found a way to stay alive under desperate circumstances while fighting the elements. The most famous *útilegumenn* are the eighteenth-century couple Fjalla-Eyvindur and Halla – Iceland's answer to Bonnie and Clyde. While there is no indication that they did anything worse than stealing food to survive, and were known to have helped lost travellers, the couple spent decades in the Highlands on the run from justice. Today, you can visit several caves and small crevasses that they used for shelter, for example, at Hveravellir in the centre of Iceland and at Herðubreiðarlindir towards the northeast. It is hard to comprehend how they managed to survive an Icelandic winter, let alone volcanic eruptions like the one in Laki in 1783 that sent an ash cloud over Iceland, causing a great famine that killed around a quarter of the population. The cloud hung over the Northern Hemisphere for months, and it has even been suggested that the eruption indirectly contributed to the French Revolution in 1789, as it led to poor harvests in Europe in subsequent years.

Hekla is Iceland's most famous and active volcano. It erupts quite regularly, and for centuries it was believed to be the gateway to hell. The mountain was first ascended in 1750 by two natural scientists who proved that there was nothing to be found at the top except a wonderful view. A slightly more infamous volcano made its mark internationally in 2010. Eyjafjallajökull's eruption resulted in a huge ash cloud covering Europe and halting all air traffic for several days. More than 100,000 flights were cancelled because of the eruption, impacting millions of travellers.

The Highlands can easily give you the impression that you are on the Moon, and indeed, Iceland's lunar-like landscape was NASA's training ground for the 1969 moon landings. Their main training ground at Nautagil ('bull's valley), isn't named after bulls, but after Neil Armstrong and all the other astro-*nauts* who trained there. Today, the Highlands are still used for space preparation – most recently for missions to Mars.

The intense beauty of the glaciers can be surreal – or as the Nobel laureate Halldór Laxness once said in his book *World Light* (*Heimsljós*), 'Where the glacier meets the sky, the land ceases to be earthly, and the earth becomes one with the heavens'). The glaciers are vast stretches of ice as far as the eye can see, with deep crevasses where their 'tongues' start to break off and descend down the valleys. As the ice is slowly moving from the centre to the extremities, an object that falls into a crevasse will eventually be 'returned' by the glacier. Parts of an airplane that crashed in Gígjökull during the Second World War are now being returned, crushed by the ice. Vatnajökull, literally 'the glacier of waters', is Europe's biggest glacier mass and also the location of Iceland's highest peak, Hvannadalshnjúkur, at 2,110 metres (6,922 feet).

Exploring glaciers is popular amongst the most adventurous, on foot or skis, or in jeeps or snowmobiles, particularly in spring when the days are longer and

the crevasses are covered with snow bridges, making them less dangerous than in summer. If you are planning to take a glacier trip, *always* go with an experienced guide and have the right equipment, such as ice crampons, an ice axe and a helmet (see page 125).

We recommend Skaftafell, south of Vatnajökull, where you can see glacier tongues coming down from the top. If you are a hiker, the walk up to Kristínartindar is beautiful and will give you a stunning view over the glacier. Further east, you'll find Jökulsárlón, a glacial lagoon where you can sail next to icebergs that are breaking off Vatnajökull.

What (Not) To Do in the Highlands

Icelandic nature is extremely fragile, particularly in the Highlands. Visitors must be very careful not to leave their mark, as the damage caused can be visible for decades. Icelanders are *extremely* passionate about protecting nature, so seeing behaviour such as someone throwing a cigarette butt out a window, tearing up moss, scratching their names onto rocks or lava, picking up stones as souvenirs, or driving off-road just breaks our hearts.

Travelling in the Highlands can require crossing unbridged rivers, so you need a good four-wheel-drive car. Most rental companies will not allow you to take your car to the Highlands, as it is important to know the conditions and how to deal with them. It is also important to know that there are absolutely no service stations there – no petrol pumps or shops whatsoever. There's nothing but mountain roads and the occasional hut or rescue shelter for travellers. Roads can sometimes look easily passable as you start, but soon become very difficult to navigate unless you are well-equipped and knowledgeable. Crossing the interior is absolutely not a shortcut.

Two roads cross Iceland from south to the north: Kjölur and Sprengisandur. These roads, like other mountain roads, don't open until well into the summer, as they are gravel and need to dry completely before cars are allowed to cross. Otherwise they can get damaged and cars may get stuck. Always respect road closures.

It is extremely important to stay on the road and not ever be tempted to drive off it, even to overtake someone or to let another car pass. The vegetation is very vulnerable and tyre marks can stay there for decades. There is a hefty fine for off-road driving and Icelanders urge people who see someone doing it to film the incident and send the footage to the police.

How To Behave in the Highlands
- Don't drive off-road.
- Don't pick up moss or other vegetation.
- Don't take stones to bring home as souvenirs.
- Don't throw anything into hot springs or geothermal pools.
- Don't leave anything behind (any litter whatsoever, even toilet paper).
- If you open a gate, always close it behind you. This stops sheep wandering too far into the highlands and ending up in a completely different part of the country by autumn.
- Always respect closed areas (such as bird sanctuaries during hatching season).

Reykjavík

Reykjavík is the world's northernmost capital city – and with just over 230,000 inhabitants in the larger metropolitan area, it is also one of the smallest. However, it punches well above its weight. Vibrant culture, an exciting music scene, excellent restaurants and heaving nightlife make it much more dynamic than a typical city or town of the same size elsewhere.

Reykjavík is a city of contrasts. Colourful corrugated iron-clad houses nestled together in the old town make the centre of Reykjavík look like a quaint little fishing village – but it is also cut through by motorways that seem borrowed from a much larger city. There are leafy neighbourhoods, but also more austere suburbs with low-rise concrete blocks scattered around lava fields. However, wherever you find yourself in Reykjavík, nature is never far away, with its rugged coastline, coves and beaches, lush valleys and forests all framed by the imposing backdrop of Mount Esja.

Visitors to Iceland often don't give Reykjavík much of a chance, preferring to head straight out to the spectacular landscapes highlighted in their guidebooks – but you should take time to explore the city. If you are lucky enough to be there on a calm and clear spring evening, as the setting sun paints the sky bright pink and lights up the majestic Snæfellsjökull glacier hovering on the horizon across the bay, you'll understand the words of a much-loved 1950s tune that most Icelanders know: 'Nothing in this world is more beautiful than a spring night in Reykjavík'.

A Very Short History of Reykjavík

According to the twelfth-century *Landnámabók* (*The Book of Settlements*), Iceland was first settled around 870 by a couple, Ingólfur Arnarson and Hallveig Fróðadóttir. The story goes that as they approached Iceland from the south, Ingólfur tossed his *öndvegissúlur* (wooden pillars that were placed either side of the seat used by the head of a household) overboard, vowing to settle wherever the gods washed them ashore. The pillars were recovered in a bay where steam rose from hot springs, prompting them to name the site of their farm '*Reykjavík*' – 'bay of smoke'. As the new arrivals had never experienced geothermal springs in their native Norway, they thought the steam was smoke.

In 2001, work on a new hotel in the old centre of Reykjavík led to the discovery of the ruins of a Viking longhouse from the tenth century, but parts of it were dated back to around the year 871, thanks to layers of ash from a known volcanic eruption in the Torfajökull glacier 200 kilometres (124 miles) away. You can visit the ruins at the Settlement Exhibition. A more recent excavation nearby has uncovered an older and larger Viking farm, possibly dating as far back as 865.

For almost a thousand years, Reykjavík remained a grouping of farms. By the eighteenth century, it had become the administrative centre of rule from Denmark. In the 1750s, the local sheriff, Skúli Magnússon, known as the 'Father of Reykjavík', built weaving, tanning and wool-dyeing factories in the 'village', laying the foundations for the first town in Iceland. You can still see one of Skúli's buildings in the centre of Reykjavík. Built in 1762, the modest timber building at number 10 Aðalstræti is the city's oldest house.

In 1843, Reykjavík became the seat of parliament and a hundred years later in 1944, the capital of the independent republic of Iceland. Reykjavík grew exponentially in the twentieth century, with huge migration to the city from the countryside (*á mölina*, as it was termed – 'onto the gravel'). From a village of 6,000 people in 1900, Reykjavík had become a town of almost 60,000 by 1950. Today, almost two-thirds of Iceland's population lives in Reykjavík and its adjacent municipalities.

Twenty-Four Hours in Reykjavík

Before you start, rent a bike. Dress appropriately – always bring a weatherproof jacket and your swimwear, as you're going to get wet one way or another!

Spend the morning in the old city centre. Start with breakfast in one of the many great cafés (we recommend Reykjavík Roasters, Grái Kötturinn or Duck & Rose). Head up to Hallgrímskirkja, the largest church in Iceland that dominates the skyline. You can go up to the top of the 75-metre (246-foot) tower for an amazing view. Check out the trendy boutiques on Skólavörðustígur leading up to the church and explore the lovely residential area of Þingholtin, where the streets are named after Norse gods, and cats roam free. Visit the ducks and swans at Tjörnin ('the pond') but don't feed them bread in the summer, as it attracts seagulls that attack the ducklings. Make your way to Austurvöllur, a square where you can see Alþingi, Iceland's parliament, and visit Dómkirkjan, Reykjavík's charming cathedral. The old harbour area in Grandagarður to the north is a colourful mix of small designer boutiques, cafés, restaurants, museums and art galleries, many of them in renovated fishing sheds. Having lunch there is a great idea, for example, in The Coocoo's Nest or Kaffivagninn, Reykjavík's oldest restaurant. The area is also the departure point for whale-watching and puffin tours. The old centre is small and can be explored in a couple of hours.

After lunch, take the bike path west out to Grótta lighthouse and then along the south coast around Reykjavík Airport to Nauthólsvík beach, where you can take a swim in the Atlantic or warm up in the geothermal steam baths and hot tubs. If a late lunch is more your thing, try Nauthóll or the less upscale Bragginn, a bistro next to the beach serving street food in a restored hangar from the Second World War. You can also head up the hill to the viewing deck of Perlan ('the pearl') for a 360-degree view of the city.

You could head back to the centre at this point, but if you're still feeling strong, head east through Fossvogur and the lush wild rabbit-filled Elliðaárdalur valley and up to the suburb of Árbær. There, you can visit Árbæjarsafn, a lovely open-air museum that shows you how Icelanders used to live. Árbær also has a nice swimming pool (Árbæjarlaug). Go back the same way to Nauthólsvík, where you can head north along the Öskjuhlíð hill, through Klambratún park and down to the north coast, where you'll have beautiful views of Mount Esja and, if you are lucky, the Snæfellsjökull glacier more than 100 kilometres (62 miles) away across Faxaflói bay. End up at the spectacular Harpa concert hall.

Head back to the old harbour area for dinner. We recommend Grandi Mathöll for affordable fish and chips. There's also Flatey Pizza and Matur og Drykkur if you want traditional Icelandic food with a twist. The old city centre is full of bars and clubs, often playing live music. Check out the weekly listings in the English-language *Reykjavík Grapevine* newspaper. Before you stumble home, don't forget to stop at the mythical Bæjarins beztu for the 'city's best' hot dogs. It stays open late at weekends.

Reykjavík Recommendations

Swimming pools: Vesturbæjarlaug for hanging out in the hot tubs with Reykjavík's literati, art-deco Sundhöllin and the largest complex at Laugardalslaug. Good pools for kids, for instance, are Lágafellslaug in Mosfellsbær and the pool in western Kópavogur. They both have lots of waterslides, a paddling pool with a small slide and also an indoor pool.

Museums: Reykjavík Art Museum, the National Gallery, National Museum, Reykjavík Maritime Museum, Wonders of Iceland and Planitarium (both at Perlan), the Saga Museum and Whales of Iceland. There are many smaller art museums and the Icelandic Phallological Museum if you fancy something very different.

Parks and green areas: Elliðaárdalur recreational area and salmon river; Laugardalur (Hot Spring Valley), where you'll find a family park and petting zoo, as well as a botanical garden; Öskjuhlíð, where you'll find interesting remains from the Second World War; the Grótta coastal area and lighthouse; Heiðmörk forest conservation area; and the neighbouring Rauðhólar, a cluster of red-coloured pseudocraters (non-eruptible volcanoes). Hiking up Mount Esja is easily done from Reykjavík – there is even a city bus you can take to get there.

Shopping: Skólavörðustígur and Laugavegur for small boutiques. For big brands, head to the Kringlan or Smáralind shopping malls.

Restaurants and cafés: Snaps Bistro, Sæta svínið, Apótek, Austur-Indíafjelagið, Public house, Grillmarkaðurinn, Fiskfélagið, Rok, Kol, Kopar, Forréttabarinn, Kaffi Vest (also known as Kaffihús Vesturbæjar) and Kaffitár.

Nightlife and music: Húrra, Kaldi, Veður, Prikið, Ölstofan, Dillon, and Harpa.

WHAT MAKES THE ICELANDERS

Living With the Elements

The Icelandic outlook on life is greatly shaped by the natural elements. In Iceland, we are constantly reminded that the human being is tiny compared to the gigantic forces of nature. We know that sometimes there is absolutely nothing you can do but wait until a storm passes or a road is cleared of snow. At any time you can expect an earthquake to shake things up – or indeed a volcanic eruption.

Perhaps knowing how small we are has given us the gift of not taking ourselves too seriously. We are not afraid of trying new things and are very good at learning and adapting to change. For example, when the weather is good, we'll rush out immediately to finish painting the fence or collect the hay. We don't worry about having our coffee break or how many hours of sleep we'll get. If a job needs doing, we just get it done!

Icelanders are used to having a lot of space with nothing blocking the view. Most of us see the sea and mountains every day and we can go and be completely alone in nature with no living creature in sight if we just drive for half an hour. Maybe that's why we think the sky's the limit and that opportunities are there to go after.

Over the centuries, life in Iceland has been difficult. Our genes have made it through famine, hardship and lots of bad weather. We stick together through thick and thin. If an Icelander is doing well overseas, we are all very proud. When the Icelandic men's team played in the finals of the UEFA European Football Championship in 2016 – the smallest country ever to make it that far – the whole country stood behind 'our boys'. A staggering 10 per cent of Iceland's inhabitants travelled to France to support them with the 'Viking Thunder Clap' (see page 52). When we all get together, anything is possible!

Þetta Reddast (THEH-ta RED-ast)

If Iceland had a phrase that summed up the population's attitude to life, it would certainly be 'þetta reddast' – which roughly translates as 'everything will work out in the end'.

Throughout centuries of hunger, poverty, natural disasters and endless harsh winters, Icelanders have learned to approach life's challenges with a combination of self-reliance, stoic acceptance of fate and a dash of optimism.

Icelanders today, with their geothermally heated homes, general comfort and high standard of living, have come a long way from their ancestors who battled the elements from turf huts, but a 2017 poll conducted by the University of Iceland found that nearly half of Icelanders report living their lives according to þetta reddast, proof that it is still a relevant and needed philosophy for modern life.

Over half of the survey's respondents also confirmed feeling 'very' or 'rather lucky'. So, for the modern descendants of those who survived – and even managed to thrive – against all the odds on this harsh island in the middle of the north Atlantic, everything *did* kind of work out all right in the end.

When To Use Þetta Reddast

You call an Icelandic farmer in spring to book a holiday house on his land in the summer and he tells you he has the perfect thing for you – but it just hasn't been built yet. You ask if he's sure it will be ready on time and he goes, 'Don't worry, þetta reddast!' And it actually all works out according to plan.

Where Everybody Knows Your Name

If you ask an Icelander if they have ever met Björk, they'll probably tell you they are actually related to her or went to school with someone from her family. It's not unusual to see the president or prime minister standing on the sidelines of their kids' football matches like any other parents and taking their turn at grilling the hot dogs.

Iceland's population is very small, but there are some surprising benefits to fewer numbers – which might even help to explain why Iceland consistently ranks amongst the top-five happiest countries in the world.

Social relationships with friends and family are relatively easy to maintain, especially as the majority of the population lives in the Reykjavík area. This closeness means that there is more cohesion and less social isolation than in most countries – arguably fewer people fall between the cracks. Solidarity at the national level is also very strong, whether it's coming together when times are tough or to celebrate achievements.

When there are so few people, each and every individual matters. If someone wants to be heard, they can be. Access to the media or to people in power has always been relatively easy; and with the rise of social media, a short tweet or an online post can shine the spotlight on an issue and have a direct impact on decision-making at the highest levels. In 2020, a mother posted online about her son having to change schools after being bullied. The whole country rallied around to show the boy that bullying isn't acceptable. He received supportive calls from a government minister, the captain of the national football team, pop stars and celebrities.

Opportunities are also endless for those ready to seize them. In a small society, there is always a need for talented people. Competition is less fierce and the safety net is strong, which means people aren't afraid to try different things and don't feel that they are stuck on a particular career path. You will often find Icelanders having unconventional and non-linear careers, with many going back to school in their middle age to retrain for a new profession.

There are high levels of trust as well. Children, even in Reykjavík, can move around freely and play outside without adult supervision. You'll see young children walking alone to school on dark winter mornings and babies sleeping in prams on the pavement outside cafés. If your car is stuck in snow, rest assured someone will always stop to pull you out.

Smallness is fundamental to Icelandic happiness, but it is also a collective enterprise, allowing people to not just feel safe, but to also be in control of their own lives.

How To Do the 'Viking Thunder Clap'

Rarely have Icelanders made as much noise as when we made it to the semi-final of UEFA Euro 2016 and the 'Viking Thunder Clap', performed by our passionate supporters, was heard around the world. Here's how to do it:

1. Assemble a large group of people who are all passionate about the same thing and want to intimidate the hell out of an adversary.
2. Find a tall person and a strong drummer to put up front.
3. Following the drummer's lead, do a double-clap, raise your arms and shout a loud '*húh*' ('*hoo*') in unison. Start off slowly, gradually building the pace until you have a massive wall of threatening sound.
4. Watch in delight as your adversary runs away.

Work Makes a Man Worthy

'*Vinnan göfgar manninn*' ('work makes a man worthy') is a popular Icelandic saying. The idea of working hard is deeply rooted in our culture and is probably a remnant of centuries of living and labouring in a harsh terrain, as well as the Protestant belief that the way to heaven is through hard work. Recently, efforts have been made to shorten the working week from 40 hours to as little as 36, but the average working week in Iceland is still longer than that of any other country in Western Europe (44 hours in 2019) and it is not unusual for people to have more than one job.

It is also generally accepted that it is good for children to participate in the labour market from an early age. Until only a few decades ago, the school year was organised around farm work: school ended at the beginning of May so children could participate in the lambing season, only restarting in mid-September after the sheep-gathering. Nowadays, young people are encouraged to find work during the summer holidays and some, especially those aged 15 years and older, also work throughout the school year. It is not uncommon to see teenagers at supermarket checkouts or in fish factories. In 2018, one in four children under the age of 18 was involved in the job market.

In Reykjavík, 13–16-year-olds are guaranteed employment for three weeks in the summer by the municipality, working for up to seven hours a day. The programme, which exists in a number of areas around the country, is called *Vinnuskóli* ('work school'). It teaches teenagers basic professional skills such as sticking to a routine, punctuality and taking responsibility for tasks.

The work mostly includes gardening in parks and for senior citizens. Places at *Vinnuskóli* are much sought after, but the intensity of the work is debatable. It's not uncommon to see teenagers napping in a flowerbed on a sunny afternoon or resting on their shovels while chatting with friends. The activities are, however, seen as an important first step into the world of work.

A Paradise for Women (and Men)?

In 2020, for the 11th year running, the World Economic Forum named Iceland the most gender-equal country in the world, having closed almost 88 per cent of its overall gender gap. Gender equality has become a part of the social fabric in Iceland. This did not happen overnight, but is the result of decades of struggle by strong women and feminist movements – a collective effort of society and politics to create a more gender-equal environment. Icelanders are proud of the success that has been achieved, but also mindful that the battle is not, and possibly never will be, fully 'won', as ensuring a gender equal society is a continuous task.

Perhaps the key to Iceland's success is not least that Icelanders have come to discover the benefits of equality for everyone, not only for women. It is about making sure that people, regardless of gender, can have the same opportunities. Engaging men and boys in the promotion of equality and as agents of change is crucial.

The first time Iceland found itself in the spotlight on the topic of gender equality was in 1975 (a year the United Nations had decided to dedicate to women). On Friday, 24 October, Icelandic women walked away from all their duties and took to the streets to demand gender equality. They didn't show up for work and refused to do any housework. It was called *Kvennafrí* – the 'women's day off'. It is said that many men changed their children's nappies for the first time that day, and that many families ate hot dogs or yoghurt for dinner. The strike had an enormous impact. The country came to a halt, as all the services women provided had stopped. Iceland was a very different society in 1975, but the women's day off heralded a new era.

The strike has been repeated a few times since. On those occasions, women stopped working at the time of day when they were no longer being paid according to the gender pay gap at each time. In 2005, this was at 2.08 p.m. Five years later in 2010, it was at 2.25 p.m. In 2016, women left work at 2.38 p.m.; and in 2018, at 2.55 p.m. This shows how the gender pay gap is slowly getting smaller, and there are hopes that it can be completely eliminated with obligatory equal pay certification that came into force in 2018, obliging companies and institutions that employ 25 people or more to meet the requirements of the Equal Pay Standard.

Another important milestone was the creation in 1983 of the Women's Alliance, an all-female political party. Largely due to the Alliance, the number of women in parliament jumped from five to 15 per cent in the elections that year. During its 17 years of existence, the Women's Alliance changed general public attitudes, the discourse about the role of women, and created an understanding that more women were needed at the helm of society. The number of women on Reykjavík city council went from 20 to 53.3 per cent and the number of female parliamentarians rose from five to 25 per cent.

In 2009, Jóhanna Sigurðardóttir became not only Iceland's first female prime minister but also the world's first openly gay leader. Her cabinet was the first to have an equal number of male and female ministers.

However, in the 2017 election, there was a drop in the number of women MPs – a reminder never to assume gender equality has been reached. Following that election, Iceland saw its second female prime minister, Katrín Jakobsdóttir, take office, with five out of eleven ministers in her cabinet being female at the time of writing. There are many other important posts occupied by women too, such as the Church of Iceland being led by a female bishop.

Perhaps a unique feature of Icelandic society is that it combines the highest female workforce participation in the Organisation for Economic Co-operation and Development (OECD) (77.3 per cent in 2019, with an OECD average of 53.1 per cent) with a relatively high fertility rate (1.7 children born per woman; the EU average, for example, is 1.5). You might be wondering how is this possible. The answer is that a good system has been put in place over the years, consisting of long parental leave, where people enjoy the same rights regardless of gender, with affordable and accessible day care, and a strong emphasis on shared parental responsibilities. Raising children is also seen as a family effort, with grandparents and even neighbours helping out.

Parental leave is 12 months. Each parent is entitled to six months of leave, with six weeks transferrable to the other parent, so one parent can take 7.5 months and the other 4.5 months. In certain cases, such as when single women become mothers with the help of a sperm donor, or when it has not been possible to identify the father, rights can be transferred to the other parent. This ensures that both parents take full part in the care of their children during the first months, and it helps to create a more equal distribution of domestic tasks right from the start. This has had a groundbreaking effect on gender equality and has also allowed men to be more engaged as fathers and have fuller family lives. Employers also understand that both women and men have parental responsibilities, so it is frowned upon to organise meetings after 4 p.m., and there is an understanding that parents sometimes need to stay at home with their children.

In addition, there are gender quotas for company boards and public committees, while gender-responsive budgeting has been introduced at the municipal and state level and a special emphasis given to eliminating gender-based violence.

President Vigdís Finnbogadóttir

In 1980, Vigdís Finnbogadóttir was elected president of Iceland and became the first democratically elected female head of state in the world. It was also considered newsworthy that she was a single mother. She moved into Bessastaðir (the presidential residence) with her eight-year-old daughter. Vigdís made an enormous impact on the Icelanders who grew up with her as their head of state. Girls saw they could achieve anything they aspired to, while boys realised that women could be great leaders. In 1996, when Vigdís left the presidency after 16 years, children would even ask if men could become presidents, as they were so used to seeing a woman in this high office.

The Icelandic Language

If you ever get the chance to fly an Icelandic airline and touch down at Keflavík Airport, pay close attention to the landing announcement. While passengers receive a standard welcome speech (and perhaps a weather warning!) in English, the flight attendant utters two words in Icelandic: '*Velkomin heim*' ('welcome home'). The assumption is that if you understand those words immediately, then you are indeed 'home'.

The Icelandic language is a fundamental part of the country's national identity, which the people of Iceland take great pride in and great care to preserve.

Icelandic is spoken by less than half a million people in total, most of them living in Iceland, and is not dissimilar to Old Norse, the language spoken in medieval times across Scandinavia. In fact, due to Iceland's geographical isolation and more recent efforts to preserve it, Icelandic has not changed all that much since the ninth and tenth centuries when the island was first settled. Icelanders will love to tell you that they can pick up an 800-year-old manuscript and read it fluently. This is definitely an exaggeration, but it is true that, if transcribed into modern spelling, the average Icelander could make their way through the text quite easily.

Icelandic is sometimes referred to as 'the Latin of the North', as it is still much closer to the original language of the Vikings than other Nordic languages such as Danish, Swedish or Norwegian. As Vikings travelled widely, they left an influence on other languages, particularly in words that relate to farming and fighting. Can you guess the English meaning of *gras, hey, kross, blóð, bátur,*

skip, víkingur, heiðinn, steik, rotinn, tröll, saga, berserkur and *traust*? (Grass, hay, cross, blood, boat, ship, Viking, heathen, steak, rotten, troll, saga, berserk and trust).

Beware the Language Police

It was in the eighteenth century that the push to preserve the purity of the Icelandic language began. Icelandic had by then absorbed elements from other languages, especially Danish.

The effort was largely instigated by Eggert Ólafsson (1726–68), an Icelandic explorer and writer. Eggert (we all go by first names in Iceland, as you'll see in the 'Family Life and Life's Milestones' chapter, see page 168) was well-read in medieval Icelandic literature and was passionate about his language and culture. Along with many poems and texts, he wrote the first orthographical dictionary for Icelandic in an effort to standardise spelling.

The linguistic purity movement continued to gain momentum, and is still very much alive today, with efforts to keep the language true to its ancient roots, but equally relevant in the modern world. Instead of adopting loan words, as languages such as English and French often do, Icelanders have chosen to get creative and develop their own. For example, the word 'computer' clearly did not exist in medieval times, so when the first computer came to Iceland in 1964 a new term had to be created – *tölva*. The word is a rather ingenious hybrid of *tala* (number) and *völva* (a female oracle). The literal definition of a computer in Icelandic is, therefore, 'a numerical oracle'! *Tölva* was a huge improvement from the mouthful *rafeindareiknir*, which had been used temporarily up to then, and caught on immediately. So while Icelanders sometimes joke about 'the language police', words such as *sjónvarp* ('vision-broadcast') and *gervitungl* ('fake-moon') will always be used over 'TV' and 'satellite'.

The fact that Icelandic has prevailed for as long as it has, and stood the test of time and foreign influence, shows just how important the language is to the overall identity of the nation. Icelanders also realise that it is up to them to safeguard Icelandic – because nobody else will do it for them.

The Icelandic Alphabet

Icelandic is a very phonetic language, so when you've learned how to pronounce its 32 letters, you can say words easily. The stress is always on the first syllable and there are no silent letters.

Aa Áá Bb Dd Ðð Ee Éé Ff Gg Hh Ii Íí Jj Kk Ll Mm Nn Oo Óó Pp Rr Ss Tt Uu Úú Vv Xx Yy Ýý Þþ Ææ Öö

Note that there is no C, Q, W or Z. All the regular vowels (A, E, I, O, U, plus Y) have an identical vowel with what looks like an accent over it. However, these aren't accents at all – they signify a different vowel with a different sound. In addition, there are two more vowels: Æ and Ö. In total, there are 14 vowels and 18 consonants.

The two letters most non-native speakers struggle with in Icelandic are Ð ('*eth*') and the Þ ('*thorn*'), along with the rolled R. They used to be found in various languages, including Old English, but today, Icelandic and Faroese are the only living languages that use Ð, while Þ is unique to Icelandic.

Ð looks like a D with a line through it when capitalised, and is sometimes confused for an ó in its lowercase form ð. In fact, the letter sounds identical to the 'th' in the English words 'the', 'they' or 'then'.

Þ appears in many words, most notably in Þingvellir, the site of Iceland's ancient parliament. This is not a P, so don't pronounce Þingvellir as 'Pingvellir'. Þ is pronounced like the 'th' in the English words 'thing' or 'think', so an acceptable way to write Þ if you don't have it on your keyboard is 'th', as in 'Thingvellir'.

Pronunciation tip: Ð uses the vocal cords, while Þ just involves blowing air between your tongue and teeth!

Breaking It Down

Icelandic is infamous for being one of the hardest languages to learn, and this is true. With its complex grammar, strange letters and tongue-twisting pronunciation, constructing a correct sentence can feel like a form of mental gymnastics. However, those who get past these initial difficulties will find that Icelandic words are often incredibly simple and transparent, with many made up of a combination of smaller words.

In 2010, the volcanic eruption at the Eyjafjallajökull glacier and the resulting cloud of ash brought air travel in Europe and across the Atlantic to a standstill – and gave newsreaders around the world a headache. How on earth could '*Eyjafjallajökull*' be a word? Well, it's one of those words that consists of three separate ones. *Eyja* means 'island', *fjalla* are 'mountains' and *jökull* means 'glacier'. Basically, Eyjafjallajökull means 'islandmountainglacier'. Not so daunting anymore.

Due to these compound words, Icelandic can be a very transparent language. *Ljósmóðir* ('mother of light') is a midwife and has been selected the most beautiful word in Icelandic, *hugmynd* ('mind picture') is an idea, *ljósmynd* ('light picture') is a photograph, and so on.

Icelanders like to play around with word combinations, stringing them together to create extremely long words. The longest word to date in Icelandic is *Vaðlaheiðarvegavinnuverkfærageymsluskúrslyklakippuhringurinn*. It means 'the keyring to the tool shed of the roadworks of Vaðlaheiði' (Vaðlaheiði is a mountain road in north Iceland).

How To Pretend To Speak Icelandic

Icelandic is not an easy language to learn, but one extremely versatile word can get you far: *jæja* (pronounced yEYE-ya). Its equivalent in English would probably be 'well' or 'so', but that doesn't fully capture the infinite potential of *jæja*.

Jæja! – Let's go!
Jæja? – Are you coming?
Jæja. – I'm bored.
Jæja! ... – That's enough now ...
Jæja? – What's up?
Jæja! – Ah, that makes sense!
Jæja? – Really?
Jæja? – What's the problem?
Jæja. – That was disappointing.
Jæja ... – I have nothing to say, but want to fill the silence ...
Jæja. – We'll figure it out.

Green Iceland

What do locally grown tomatoes, heated swimming pools, aluminium, cosmetic products rich in silica, snow-free driveways and clean air have in common? These are all things for which Icelanders can thank an abundance of renewable energy sources.

Iceland is sometimes (and quite rightly) referred to as 'the land of fire and ice'. Indeed, 10 per cent of the country is covered with glaciers, and volcanic eruptions take place every few years. However, that ice and fire have, over time, become Iceland's 'gold' – sources of renewable energy that Icelanders have learned to harness, making the country a role model for others when it comes to sustainability and the transition from fossil fuels to renewable energy.

Today, all stationary energy use (i.e. all needs for electricity and heating) in Iceland is met by renewable energy sources, making it a world leader in the use of renewable energy. The only sector that still depends on fossil fuel is transport (including fisheries). Iceland's aim is to be carbon-neutral by 2040, so Icelanders are working on switching to carbon-free transport and increasing carbon capture and storage. In 2020, 25 per cent of all new registered cars were completely electric, making Iceland the second country in the world (after Norway) when it comes to the share of sales of new cars that are running on electricity. If plug-in hybrid and methane-fuelled cars are included, the number goes up to 58 per cent.

Iceland's unique story of how it became a leader in renewable energy started more than a century ago, and in less than a generation its energy system was transformed. The first hydroelectric power station started operating in 1904; today, hydropower accounts for 75 per cent of Iceland's electricity production. The run-off water from snow and glaciers melting in the summer is captured in reservoirs and fed through rivers to the power plants, creating clean energy on its way to the ocean. By storing the water in summer and controlling the flow from the reservoirs over the year, it is possible to adapt to energy demands at any given time. It is almost like having a huge battery. Of course, much more energy is needed in the cold, dark winter than in summer, and during the winter the glaciers accumulate snow that then melts and feeds into the reservoir the following summer.

The other 25 per cent of the electricity comes from below the ground in the form of geothermal power. For centuries, Icelanders have used geothermal springs for washing, cooking, cleaning and bathing (quite useful for a country called Iceland to have such an abundance of heat). In 1908, steam was first

used for heating and indoor cooking by a creative farmer who installed pipes to run it from a nearby hot spring. Harnessing geothermal energy for space heating started on an industrial level in 1930 and the first power plants came into existence in the late 1960s.

The use of domestic renewable energy has had an immense benefit to Icelanders, increasing quality of life with warm houses, electricity, an abundance of swimming pools and even heated pavements and town squares. It has also diversified the economy and attracted industries such as aluminium and ferro-silicon production. Renewables have made Iceland more self-reliant when it comes to food production, as some vegetables are grown in heated greenhouses all year-round, and fruits such as raspberries, blackberries and strawberries are cultivated for part of the year.

Very few Icelanders know that up until only half a century ago Iceland was considered to be a developing country by the United Nations Development Programme. Harnessing natural energy sources gave it a huge economic boost, in addition to the environmental benefits.

Iceland places a big emphasis on helping countries utilise renewable energy sources. It runs the Geothermal Training Programme in association with UNESCO, and more than 700 geothermal experts from more than 60 countries have been trained since its launch in 1979. Icelandic companies have participated in renewable energy projects in countries as varied as China, Chile, Djibouti, Ethiopia, Georgia, Greenland, Kenya and Nicaragua, so Iceland's expertise is contributing to fighting climate change on a global scale. New and innovative solutions are also being developed to reduce the impact of climate change, such as the Carbfix technology of binding captured carbon dioxide (CO_2) into rock, where it naturally mineralises and is permanently stored. Plans are underway to start transporting CO_2 from overseas for permanent mineral storage in Iceland's basaltic bedrock.

Iceland's contribution to fighting climate change is multifaceted and goes way beyond Iceland itself. Not only has Iceland transformed its energy system and greatly reduced its own emissions, but it is also using its green energy to make energy-intensive products for exports (like aluminium) and thus reducing CO_2 emissions worldwide. As a nation, it is also helping other countries to make use of their own potential for renewable energy – not a small contribution to fighting the greatest environmental challenge of our time.

CULTURE

Blind Is a Man Without a Book

In many countries, cultural heritage is reflected in ancient castles, temples, cathedrals or other great monuments. Iceland's cultural heritage lies in books and old manuscripts. Such manuscripts describe the settlement of Iceland, the first settlers and where they lived, as well as other parts of our history. Literary works such as the *Edda* are an important source of knowledge about ancient Norse mythology.

It is the sagas that are Iceland's most important contribution to world literature. They were written in the thirteenth and fourteenth centuries, on calfskin, and describe events that took place between the ninth and eleventh centuries. In total, there are about 40 sagas preserved. Some of the most famous include *Laxdæla saga*, *Njáls saga* and *Egils saga*. They tell the stories of people that really did exist and are written in a very straightforward fashion, describing a world of conflict, vengeance, love, friendship and honour. These tales have been read and told by generation after generation in Iceland, and have forged our cultural identity.

Despite its historical material poverty, Iceland has always had a very high literacy rate, and books were considered as important possessions (not all Icelanders realised the importance of old manuscripts though, as pages were sometimes torn out to fill gaps in walls to stop the wind coming in, or even to make sewing patterns). Sayings such as '*Blindur er bóklaus maður*' ('blind is a man without a book') and '*Betra er berfættum en bókarlausum að vera*' ('better to be barefoot than without books') show their importance in Iceland. Some of the first foreign visitors described in their written journals the astonishment of finding a poor farmer in some remote valley stepping out of his turf house and welcoming them in fluent Latin.

Reading and storytelling is simply part of our DNA. Today's Icelanders read an average of 2.3 books each month, according to a recent study, and it is sometimes said that one in 10 Icelanders will write a book in their lifetime. Reading books is almost a national sport! *Kiljan*, one of the most popular TV shows, is all about literature, including interviews with authors, reviews about recently published books, and digging into Iceland's literary heritage. Reykjavík was also designated as a UNESCO City of Literature in 2011.

CULTURE

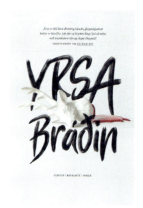

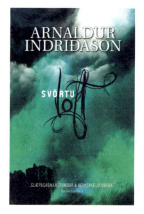

However, narrative literature barely existed for many centuries in Iceland, perhaps because of extreme poverty, although writing verse and poetry continued. The Nobel Prize in Literature was awarded to author Halldór Laxness in 1955, making him a national hero and strengthening Icelanders' confidence in their literary output. It confirmed that Iceland, which had become fully independent from Denmark only 11 years before, had something to contribute to world literature beyond the sagas.

Halldór was a very prolific author who displayed a profound understanding of Icelanders' nature, for example in his novel *Independent People* (*Sjálfstætt fólk*).

More recently, and despite coming from one of the safest countries in the world, Icelandic crime fiction has gained a large international following. Arnaldur Indriðason, Yrsa Sigurðardóttir and Ragnar Jónasson are good authors to start with if you want to explore this genre. Other prize-winning writers of contemporary fiction, who have gained international acclaim, include Jón Kalman Stefánsson, Auður Ava Ólafsdóttir, Gerður Kristný, Hallgrímur Helgason, Sigríður Hagalín Björnsdóttir, Andri Snær Magnason and Sjón.

The Christmas Book Flood

Christmas without a new book to read is unimaginable for Icelanders. It is like Easter without chocolate. A long-standing tradition is that everyone should receive at least one new book under the tree on Christmas Eve, the night is often spent snuggled up in bed reading.

Given this strong tradition of giving and receiving books at Christmas, it is not surprising that the majority of new publications arrive in the autumn, just in time for the holiday season. New books *flood* the market, newspapers review them, and authors compete for interviews. Award nominations are announced, bestseller lists are published, and people flock to bookshops to have a look at the latest arrivals. This annual frenzy even has its own name, *Jólabókaflóð* – the Christmas book flood.

Bókatíðindi, or the 'book bulletin', is a catalogue listing all the new titles by category, which is published annually and distributed to every home in Iceland. The arrival of the bulletin is solid proof that Christmas is around the corner. People read it with excitement and mark the titles they are putting on their wish lists, or want to give to their loved ones.

Idioms

Related to Agriculture

Allt gengur á afturfótunum: 'Everything's walking on its hind legs'. Something isn't going well.
'Ever since we started this new project, everything has been walking on its hind legs and no progress has been made!'

Að hlaupa undir bagga: 'To run under a bale of hay'. In the old days, horses were used to move hay. The idiom makes reference to if a bale was about to drop, someone would help out by running under it to stop the fall.
'I need to work late, so I'm going to see if my parents can run under the bale of hay and collect the kids from football practice.'

Áfram með smjörið: 'On with the butter'. Similar to 'onwards and upwards'. This idiom makes reference to the process of churning milk to make butter.

Related to Fishing

Að leggja árar í bát: 'To put the oars in the boat'. To give up.
'He had tried to learn to play the piano, but in the end, he put the oars in the boat'.

Vera eins og þorskur á þurru landi: 'To be like cod on dry land'. To be out of place or not fit in.

Vera eins og síld í tunnu: 'To be like herring in a barrel'. Iceland's version of 'packed in like sardines'.

'So many people attended the concert that it was like being a herring in a barrel. But that was OK because *þröngt mega sáttir sitja* – good friends can sit tightly.'

Koma heim með öngulinn í rassinum: 'To come home with the fishing hook in your arse'. This colourful reference is about failing at something – such as returning from a fishing trip with no catch.

Related to Elves and Trolls

Að vera eins og álfur út úr hól: 'To be like an elf outside its hill'. Not belonging or fitting in somewhere.

Vera týndur og tröllum gefinn: 'To be lost and given to the trolls'. To have disappeared for good.

'I took my coat to school yesterday, but it is lost and given to the trolls. I can't find it anywhere.'

Related to the Weather

Vita ekki hvaðan á sig stendur veðrið: 'Not to know which direction the weather is coming from'. To be taken by total surprise.

Skjótt skipast veður í lofti: 'The weather changes quickly'. Referring to a rapidly changing situation.

'The team had the upper hand, but the weather changes quickly. In the last minute, the other team scored and the game ended with a tie.'

Miscellaneous

Að kalla ekki allt ömmu sína: 'To not call everything one's grandmother'. To be brave and able to take on hardship.
'This man has done great things and certainly does not call everything his grandmother!'

Þar fór góður biti í hundskjaft: 'That was a good bite wasted in a dog's mouth'. Something good was wasted on someone who didn't deserve it.

Leggjast undir feld: 'To lie down under fur'. To think about something long and hard in order to make a decision. This idiom makes reference to Þorgeir Ljósvetningagoði, a lawman who, in the year 1000, was asked at Alþingi (the Parliament) at Þingvellir to decide if Iceland should remain pagan or become Christian. He took a big fur blanket, went to bed and stayed there until he decided Iceland should take up Christianity.

Koma af fjöllum: 'To come from the mountains'. To not know something. If you've been in the mountains, you won't be up to date with everything that's been going on.
'When asked about his opinion on the scandal in his company, the CEO said he was coming from the mountains.'

Bíta í skjaldarrendur: 'To bite the edges of the shield'. To find extra strength.
'There have been economic difficulties, but the people must bite the edges of the shield to overcome them.'

Icelandic Words That Don't Exist in English

Alnafni/alnafnar: A person who has the exact same name as you. If Jón Gunnarsson meets another Jón Gunnarsson, they are *alnafnar*. *Nafni* or *nafna* is used when you have the same first name.

Duglegur: Efficient and hardworking, particularly in a work, school, or domestic context. Being *duglegur* is a great virtue in Iceland.

Frekja: A bossy, demanding person.

Fundvís: A word describing someone who has a knack for finding lost things easily.

Gluggaveður: Weather that only looks nice if viewed from indoors through a window.

Hallærislegt: Something that is unbearably uncool.

Íslandsvinur: Someone famous who has been to Iceland.

Kjötsvimi: When you've eaten so much meat that you get all dizzy.

Kviðmágur/kviðsystir: Someone who has had the same sexual partner as you (not at the same time, though). It literally means 'abdomen-brother-in-law' for men, or 'abdomen-sister' for women.

Landkynning: 'Promotion of the country'. A drunken Icelander abroad is poor promotion for the country, for example.

Nenna: Not wanting to do something due to laziness.

Páskahret: An Easter snow storm. Just when you think winter has passed, but cold weather returns, which often happens over Easter.

Ratljóst: When there is just enough daylight for you to find your way.

Rúntur: Going for a drive around town (often in circles around the main square). Sometimes alcohol is involved (for those not in the driver's seat) and loud music. *Rúntur* can also be something to do on a date.

Rúsínurassgat: Literally 'raisin ass'. This word is used for cute children: 'Oh, look at that *rúsínurassgat*, isn't he cute?' *Rassgatarófa*, or 'asshole turnip', is also a term of endearment for cute children.

Skárra: A little bit better, but still not good.

Skreppa: To go out for a short while, often to run errands (although Icelanders are prone to understatement, so this could be for days).

Sólarhringur: Literally one 'ring' around the sun: a period of 24 hours.

Svikalogn: Calm before a storm. Literally calm (no wind) that betrays.

Svili/svilkona: The sister or brother of your brother/sister-in-law.

Trúnó: Confidential chat, often with just one person, when you open up and pour your heart out. Often after consuming alcohol.

Unglingaveiki: Literally 'teenager sickness' – the moody behaviour exhibited by teenagers.

Vesen: Something that is more complicated than it should be.

Music

You may not have known it, but you've probably listened to some Icelandic music in the past week. Music is one of Iceland's top exports and, despite the small population, the country can boast an incredible list of great bands, solo artists and composers.

You've certainly heard of Björk, the world's most famous Icelander (probably ever), but bands such as Kaleo, Sigur Rós, and Of Monsters and Men, as well as composers such as Ólafur Arnalds, Jóhann Jóhannsson, Daníel Bjarnason, and the Academy Award-winning Hildur Guðnadóttir have had enormous international success.

For centuries, there wasn't much going on musically in Iceland. Due to the isolation, developments took a long time to reach us, so music consisted mainly of a very simple medieval-style singing of poetry (*rímur*) and hymns, sometimes sung in distinctive parallel fifths (*tvísöngur*, or 'twin-song'). Well into the nineteenth century, even four-part choral singing and instrumental music were next to non-existent.

When modern music and instruments finally arrived, Icelanders proved to be very receptive. By the second half of the twentieth century, Iceland had a thriving classical music scene (with a world-class symphony orchestra and opera house), as well as pop musicians taking the world by storm.

The explosion in music production in the past few decades can largely be explained by Iceland's strong emphasis on education. Children all over the country have access to subsidised lessons and music schools are especially active outside Reykjavík. Many of the big names in Icelandic music come from small towns and villages.

The creative melting pot of Reykjavík's live music scene, where most musicians need to play in more than one band to make ends meet, has allowed for lots of interesting blends of ideas and music styles, and has been credited for the unique sound for which many Icelandic artists are renowned overseas. This was especially true in the 80s and early 90s, when Icelandic music started to gain proper international attention with bands like Mezzoforte and, most notably, The Sugarcubes and their lead singer Björk. Musical resources were scarce, resulting in a 'DIY' attitude among young musicians. Combined with a *þetta reddast* outlook (see page 48), this self-reliant and limitless approach laid the foundations for the extraordinary music scene of today.

Top Icelandic Artists To Check Out (If You Haven't Already)

Björk: World-famous for her unique music, voice and look. She undoubtedly paved the way for Icelandic musicians who came after her. Björk started off as a child star before moving on to punk in her teens. After forming Sykurmolarnir (a.k.a The Sugarcubes), the band's breakout English-language single, *Birthday*, propelled her to fame. Since releasing her first adult solo album, *Debut*, in 1993, Björk has released nine studio albums, won five Brit Awards and four MTV Video Music Awards, among many other honours. She has also been nominated for an Academy Award and 15 Grammys (the female artist with the most nominations and no wins to date).

Kaleo: A rock band made up of a group of childhood friends from Mosfellsbær, just outside Reykjavík. Kaleo have been extremely successful in the US, where their song *Way Down We Go* topped the Billboard Alternative Songs Chart, while *No Good* received a Grammy nomination for Best Rock Performance. Well known for their live performances in spectacular Icelandic nature (check out YouTube!).

Sigur Rós: The art-rock band formed in the 1990s is probably the most famous band Iceland has ever produced. Their sound is entirely unique and experimental, sometimes not even using real words in their songs; instead, utilising sounds and emotion to convey meaning, in a nonsensical language they call 'Hopelandic'. When combined with the use of a bowed guitar and the falsetto vocals of lead singer Jónsi, the sound is otherworldly.

Of Monsters and Men: The indie folk-rock band took their first steps in 2010 at *Músíktilraunir*, a battle-of-the-bands type competition in Reykjavík, which they unexpectedly won. Only a year later, *Little Talks* from their debut album *My Head is an Animal* was a top-10 hit across the world. Second album *Beneath the Skin* made it to number one in Canada and three in the US.

Ásgeir: Raised in the tiny hamlet of Laugarbakki, halfway between Reykjavík and Akureyri, singer Ásgeir's 2012 electronic-folk album *Dýrð í dauðaþögn*, where he performed lyrics written by his father, became the biggest-selling debut album ever in Iceland. *In the Silence*, the English version of the album, was released to critical acclaim in 2014 and Ásgeir has continued his career with more albums and a steady following worldwide.

Emilíana Torrini: Beautiful love songs and upbeat music, such as the 2009 hit *Jungle Drum*, have given this singer a large international fanbase. Emilíana is also known for her performance of *Gollum's Song* in the film *The Two Towers*, the second of the *Lord Of The Rings* trilogy.

Bríet: This singer-songwriter took Iceland by storm in 2020 with her debut release *Kveðja, Bríet* and the song of the year, *Rólegur kúreki* ('easy, cowboy').

Auður: Newcomer of the year at the Icelandic Music Awards in 2016, Auður has since won over Iceland with his R&B-infused electronic music.

Reykjavíkurdætur: Iceland's first all-female hip-hop group (the name means 'daughters of Reykjavík'), comprising at times of up to 19 members. They rap almost exclusively in Icelandic and the lyrics revolve mostly around the experience of being a woman in Iceland, focusing on sexuality, body-shaming, rape culture, corrupt politicians and maternity.

Ólafur Arnalds: A musician difficult to classify. He does everything, from experimental music to film scores, and is a multi-instrumentalist and a producer. To understand Ólafur's sound, his 2018 album *re:member* would be a good place to start.

Hildur Guðnadóttir: This composer has gained international fame for her film and television scores. Between 2019 and 2020 she won almost every prize imaginable (including an Emmy, a Grammy, an Academy Award, a Golden Globe and a Bafta) for her scores for the HBO miniseries *Chernobyl* and the film *Joker*.

Víkingur Ólafsson: A superstar pianist who has played with most of the world's major orchestras. His Bach recordings in 2019 won Album of the Year at the *BBC Music Magazine* Awards.

Art

One of the oldest artifacts at the National Museum of Iceland, believed to date from around 1200, is an old church door carved out of wood, from Valþjófsstaður in east Iceland. However, not much is known about Icelandic artists before the late nineteenth century. The most renowned of the old masters in Iceland is Jóhannes Kjarval. His nature paintings, in particular of the magical beauty of moss-covered lava fields, have made him one of Iceland's best-loved artists. Kjarvalsstaðir is a museum in Reykjavík that has running exhibitions of his art, in addition to established modern artists. Other important Icelandic artists from the twentieth century are Ásgrímur Jónsson, Nína Tryggvadóttir, Louisa Matthíasdóttir, Gunnlaugur Scheving, Gerður Helgadóttir and sculptors Ásmundur Sveinsson and Einar Jónsson, many of whom have museums dedicated to their art.

The contemporary art scene is thriving. There are many galleries and exhibition spaces, some established, others popping up for a few years before disappearing. We recommend, in particular, a visit to Ásmundarsalur, part of the Reykjavík Art Museum. It has fascinating exhibitions and a really cosy café. Also of particular note are i8 Gallery and Gallerí Fold, which has frequent auctions where works of the old masters sometimes change hands.

Erró was the first Icelandic painter to achieve international acclaim with his pop art in the 1960s and 70s. Ólafur Elíasson is one of the world's best known large-scale installation artists, using natural elements such as light, water and air temperature to enhance a viewer's experience. Ólafur also designed the facade of the Harpa concert hall in Reykjavík. Ragnar Kjartansson is a performance artist well-known for his video installations, live performances and drawings that incorporate the history of film, music, visual culture and literature, often with theatrical humour and tragedy. Shoplifter (a.k.a. Hrafnhildur Arnardóttir) is known for her sculptures, murals and installations using real and synthetic hair. Shoplifter represented Iceland at the Venice Biennale in 2019 with her extremely photogenic synthetic hair installation *Chromo Sapiens*.

Performing Arts, Film and TV

Icelanders love the theatre and live performance. Despite Reykjavík's relatively small population, it's home to two professional theatres: Þjóðleikhúsið (the National Theatre) and Borgarleikhúsið (Reykjavík Municipal Theatre). Between them, they stage around 30 productions each year, a mix of both original pieces and adaptations from overseas. In addition, independent theatres such as Tjarnarbíó and Vesturport are very active. Leikhópurinn Lotta, a theatre group for children, travels around Iceland in summer with outdoor performances of plays based on traditional fairy tales with a twist. The Harpa concert hall is home to the National Symphony Orchestra and the Icelandic Opera, hosting a variety of concerts and events all year round. There is also the Iceland Dance Company.

The Icelandic film scene is also very active. Iceland's only arthouse cinema, Bíó Paradís in Reykjavík, hosts a variety of film festivals throughout the year and has a great selection of independent world cinema. In 2019, 10 Icelandic feature films were premiered across Iceland, in addition to six documentaries.

Recent interesting and award-winning films are: *Hross í oss* (*Of Horses and Men*) and *Kona fer í stríð* (*Woman At War*), both directed by Benedikt Erlingsson; *Andið eðlilega* (*And Breathe Normally*) by Ísold Uggadóttir; *Hrútar* (*Rams*) by Grímur Hákonarson; *Hvítur, hvítur dagur* (*A White, White Day*) by Hlynur Pálmason; *Agnes Joy* (*Agnes Joy*) by Silja Hauksdóttir; and *Fúsi* (*Virgin Mountain*) by Dagur Kári. Iceland has also produced popular TV series, among them the 'Nordic noir' crime series *Brot* (*The Valhalla Murders*) and *Ófærð* (*Trapped*).

Only one Icelandic film, Friðrik Þór Friðriksson's *Börn náttúrunnar* (*Children of Nature*), has ever been nominated for the Academy Award for Best International Feature Film, in 1992. Over the last twenty years, there have been increasing opportunities for Icelanders to work in the film industry, as Iceland has become a popular filming location. Movies shot here include the 007 films *A View to a Kill* and *Die Another Day*, *Lara Croft: Tomb Raider*, *The Secret Life of Walter Mitty*, *Oblivion*, *Noah*, *Interstellar*, *Transformers: Age Of Extinction* and *Star Wars: The Force Awakens*, as well as the TV series *Game of Thrones*.

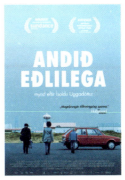

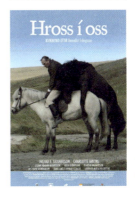

Style

Icelandic individualism and creativity is reflected in the way we dress. Reykjavík street fashion, in particular, is often very extravagant, with the most fashionable people working hard to outdo each other with the latest fashion trends, often mixed with vintage clothing and recycled pieces. The most distinctive Icelandic designers combine a focus on sustainability with references to nature and culture. Here are some names to look out for:

Aftur: A fixture of the Icelandic fashion landscape since 1999, Aftur ('again') recycle and upcycle old textiles to make unique pieces.

AndreA: Stylish women's clothing, glamorous dresses, scarves and accessories.

As We Grow: A 'slow fashion' luxury label, with a focus on sustainable, timeless and long-lasting quality, making reference to Iceland's rural past and a time when children's clothes were still made at home by hand.

Aurum: One of Iceland's leading jewellery brands. Drawing inspiration from nature, it only sources recycled and re-refined precious metals. Aurum's products are all handmade in Reykjavík. (See image above).

Farmers Market: Founded in 2005, this brand draws on tradition and Icelandic wool to create multifunctional clothing and accessories. (See image opposite left).

Hildur Hafstein: Handmade jewellery that aims to nourish the body and the soul.

Hildur Yeoman: With patterned, colourful, figure-hugging dresses, Hildur has become a favourite both with celebrities and the general population. Her work is joyful and extravagant.

Hlín Reykdal: Handmade colourful jewellery and accessories by Iceland's most popular designer. It's not an exaggeration to say that most Icelandic women own a piece by Hlín.

Kormákur og Skjöldur: Makers of high-quality vintage-style tweed menswear.

Kron: The most colourful, outlandish footwear imaginable. It would be niche in most other countries but is worn by Icelandic women of all ages.

Orrifinn Jewels: Unisex jewellery inspired by nature and everyday items such as tools.

Reykjavík Raincoats: Weather protection in all the colours of the rainbow. (See image above right).

swimslow: A sustainable swimwear brand using recycled fabrics. Their collection is named after Icelandic swimming pools.

66°North: This very well-known outdoors brand (called 66°Norður in Icelandic) is dependable and worth the investment.

Design

Icelandic interior design has flourished over the past decade, boosted both by the influx of tourists looking for unique pieces to take home and by Icelanders becoming more interested in local design. Unsurprisingly, designers take inspiration from nature, folklore and history, combining it with a cosmopolitan outlook and local materials such as wool, bone, stone and even fish skin.

Epal, Hrím and Kokka, all in the centre of Reykjavík, are good places to explore Icelandic design. Kirsuberjatréð ('the cherry tree') is a lovely shop in Reykjavík run by 10 female artists selling designs and handicrafts ranging from clothes and jewellery to baskets and mugs. Skúmaskot is another collaborative shop run by artists, while Kaolin specialises in pottery. Designers to look out for include:

Anna Thorunn: Furniture, vases, bowls and various items for the home. (See image top left).

FÓLK Reykjavík: A collective of designers making smart homeware, furniture and lifestyle products with a focus on sustainability, responsibility and transparency around the production process.

Fuzzy: You may have seen Fuzzy's trademark tiny stool made with Icelandic wool. It was first produced in 1972 and has had a resurgence in popularity in recent decades.

IHANNA HOME: Accessories with a graphic touch and a playful, functional aesthetic. (See image bottom left).

Katrín Ólína: Katrín's coat-hanger tree, designed in collaboration with Michael Young, is a classic in many Nordic homes. Her creations include textiles, furniture, jewellery, graphic art and more.

Lulla Doll by RoRo: A beautiful sleep companion for small babies and toddlers that plays soothing sounds of breathing and heartbeat and thereby imitating closeness. Parents of newborns praise Lulla for given them their sleep back, as it helps children sleep throughout the night. (See image top centre).

Reykjavík Letterpress: Beautiful cards and stationery, all made by hand.

Scintilla: A colourful collection of home textiles such as bed linen, towels, pillows and blankets. (See image top right).

Tulipop: A magical world, inhabited by fantasy creatures, inspired by nature. The collection features clothes and accessories, toys, stationery, books, lamps, mirrors and other items for the home. (See image bottom right).

Vorhús: A design collective in Akureyri, producing a wide range of homeware products.

Cultural Festivals

Iceland hosts a surprising number of art festivals that attract acclaimed international artists every year. Here's a list of some of our most notable events:

Myrkir Músíkdagar: Dark Music Days is an annual festival that takes place during the darkest time of winter, late January or early February, focusing on new Icelandic compositions and performers, as well as international artists.

HönnunarMars: DesignMarch is dedicated to local design and creation.

Barnamenningarhátíð: A festival of children's culture and arts held in Reykjavík, in April, over six days.

Aldrei fór ég suður: A rock festival in Ísafjörður in the Westfjords during Easter. The name means 'I never moved south', a reference to not living in Reykjavík.

Reykjavík Arts Festival: A multidisciplinary, biannual event held in summer, offering an ambitious selection of both Icelandic and international artists.

Skjaldborg: The Icelandic documentary festival held during the Whitsun weekend in Patreksfjörður in the Westfjords.

Secret Solstice: Music festival held in Reykjavík during the brightest period of the year, showcasing established and new emerging artists under the midnight sun.

Þjóðlagahátíð: A folk music festival in Siglufjörður, held at the start of July.

Eistnaflug: 'Flying testicles' is a heavy-metal festival held in Neskaupstaður in the Eastfjords in July.

LungA: An international art festival for young people, held in July in Seyðisfjörður.

Bræðslan: A music festival in Borgarfjörður Eystri, held in July.

Reykjavík Dance Festival: An international festival and platform for dancers and choreographers, taking place in August.

Reykjavík Jazz: Offering a variety of Icelandic and international artists in late August, early September.

Reykjavík International Literary Festival: Held biannually, often in April or September. An interesting and lively festival bringing many of the world's best authors to Iceland and highlighting both emerging and well-established Icelandic authors.

RIFF: The annual Reykjavík International Film Festival features about 100 films, both drama and non-fiction, from about 40 countries. It takes place in October and highlights independent film-making from around the world, emphasising emerging and new talent. The festival's main award is the Golden Puffin.

Iceland Airwaves: A music festival held in November in Reykjavík bringing together new and creative Icelandic talent and interesting artists from around the world.

AT THE TABLE

Fish

Walk into pretty much any restaurant in Iceland and you will find a 'fish of the day' on the menu. However basic the establishment might otherwise look, you are almost guaranteed to get a plate of tasty, freshly caught fish.

Icelanders top the world charts in fish and seafood consumption, with most people eating it at least twice a week and the most popular being haddock, cod, plaice and halibut. The population's longevity has been put down to the health benefits of the omega-3 fatty acids, vitamins and minerals found in fish.

As an island nation, nothing has historically been more vital to the livelihoods of Icelanders than fishing. Exports helped to transform Iceland from one of the poorest countries in Europe at the beginning of the nineteenth century to one of the richest today. As a tribute, pictures of fish decorate Icelandic coins, and while the country has no military, it has used its coastguard vessels to stand up to much larger nations to protect its fishing waters (see page 19).

Interestingly, fresh fish didn't become a big part of Icelanders' diets until the introduction of refrigeration and industrial fishing in the twentieth century. Before then, fish had to be preserved and consumed in dried or fermented forms.

Icelandic Specialities To Look Out For

Harðfiskur (stockfish): Dried, salted fish commonly eaten with butter as a snack. It traditionally replaced bread when access to grain was limited. *Harðfiskur* is one of the few traditional foods that is still part of our everyday diet and can be found in every shop.

Plokkfiskur (fish stew): A simple mix of white fish (usually haddock or cod), potato, onion, flour, milk and seasoning. Recently, some recipes also include ingredients like chives, curry powder, béarnaise sauce or cheese.

Humar (langoustine, also known as Icelandic lobster): Caught in the waters off the south coast, *humar* is known for its tasty, tender meat. You can find it grilled, baked, fried, or even as a pizza topping.

Lýsi (cod liver oil): Possibly the reason Icelanders didn't die out hundreds of years ago (and also possibly the reason for our many World's Strongest Man title holders). *Lýsi* was also once used to light homes – hence the name, which comes from the verb *lýsa* (to illuminate). Icelanders still consume a lot of *lýsi*, with a study showing half the population has it every day.

Lamb

Icelandic sheep have almost single-handedly kept the nation alive and warm since the first settlement, and the island still has more sheep than humans, although numbers have dropped quite dramatically in recent years. Having been so essential to our survival, sheep hold a special place in Icelanders' hearts, with many claiming that the Icelandic breed is the smartest, best-looking and tastiest in the world.

Each spring, the sheep are let out of their pens to spend the summer happily roaming the wilderness, grazing on (100 per cent organic) grass, moss, berries and Arctic herbs. Always on the lookout for newly sprouted vegetation, the sheep work their way from the lowlands to the highlands, from where they are brought down by farmers in the autumn. The result is a tender meat with a distinctively mild, almost game-like taste.

You'll find fresh lamb served in all kinds of delicious ways in Icelandic homes and restaurants, but the most distinctive way of preparing lamb is known as *hangikjöt*, or 'hung meat'. It is named after the old tradition of smoking the lamb by hanging it from the rafters in a smoking shed. The meat is smoked using birch, sometimes mixed with dried sheep dung to give it that extra kick.

Hangikjöt is usually boiled and served either hot or cold in slices. It is traditionally eaten at Christmas, usually accompanied by potatoes in a

béchamel sauce, green peas, red cabbage and *laufabrauð* (see page 198), and all year-round in schoolchildren's sandwiches.

'Can I Offer You a Fermented Ram's Testicle?'

This isn't a question you will often be asked, but as a tourist in Iceland, it is almost a given that at some point your guide will try to offer you this traditional delicacy known as *súrir hrútspungar*, along with some *hákarl* (fermented shark) and *svið* (singed and boiled sheep's head). Ideally, these will be washed down with a shot of Brennivín, a powerful schnapps-like spirit (see page 114). You should definitely give all these dishes a try, as they taste (slightly) better than they sound – but please don't swallow any nonsense about this being food that's commonly eaten in modern-day Iceland.

In the dark days before refrigeration, fresh meat was rarely available during the winter months. To survive, Icelanders had to preserve their food. Around the world, methods such as salting have been used for millennia. However, in a rather cruel twist of fate, Iceland, surrounded by a salty ocean, didn't have enough firewood or warm sunlight to produce salt in any great quantities. Instead, Icelanders had to turn to methods like pickling in fermented whey, drying, and smoking. Out of sheer necessity, every single part of an animal was preserved.

While many of the traditionally preserved foods, such as the aforementioned *hangikjöt* and *harðfiskur*, are still commonly eaten, the stranger delicacies only really appear once a year during Þorrablót, an ancient midwinter festival, to celebrate the arrival of the old month of Þorri, which was resurrected by a popular restaurant in Reykjavík in the 1960s. At these gatherings, which often include quite a bit of alcohol, it has become common practice to pay tribute to our ancestors by serving all their traditional food on wooden platters. However, some of the guests will stick to *hangikjöt and harðfiskur*.

The truth is that a tourist on a two-week visit to Iceland may very well consume more fermented ram's testicles than the average Icelander will in a lifetime.

Pulsa

In the centre of Reykjavík, pretty much midway between Alþingi (the parliament building) and the old harbour, stands a small shed with a big name: Bæjarins Beztu – 'the city's best'. Until recently, the shed faced onto an unappealing bit of wasteland, but while the whole area has been redeveloped, no one would dream of moving this culinary institution that actually lives up to its name, where you can buy undoubtedly the city's best hot dogs (*pulsa*).

Hot dogs are the unofficial national dish of Iceland and you will find them sold just about everywhere. The hot dog is mostly lamb (with a bit of pork and beef mixed in), which gives it a distinctive taste – but what sets it apart from hot dogs anywhere else in the world are the accompaniments. The Icelandic hot dog is topped with ketchup, a sweet mustard called *pylsusinnep* ('hot dog mustard'), raw white onions, crispy fried onions and *remúlaði*, a sauce made with mayonnaise, capers, mustard and herbs. There are variations: in the north, for example, they like to add red cabbage. Of course, you can pick and choose what you want, but you haven't eaten a hot dog like an Icelander until you've had 'one with everything'. Or, if you want to show off your Icelandic in the Friday-night queue at 3 a.m.: '*Eina með öllu, takk!*'

AT THE TABLE

Grilling Up a Storm

Unlike the rest of world, where people tend to wait for the arrival of warmer days to light up their barbecues, Icelanders don't have that luxury. Therefore, they have decided that it is *always* the right time and place for a barbecue.

How To BBQ Like an Icelander
1. Get yourself a sturdy barbecue – preferably a big, gas-powered one that isn't susceptible to rain and wind. While your BBQ is not in use, place something heavy on top of it to prevent the cover from flying away. After every storm, people use their neighbourhood Facebook groups to search for lost BBQ covers.
2. Place your BBQ strategically – where the wind does not blow directly into it, but rather into the face of the person doing the barbecuing.
3. That person should be the sturdiest of the group. Dress them appropriately in something warm and non-flammable, then send them outside with burgers, sausages and various marinated meats, or for the more adventurous, a whole leg of lamb or a salmon.
4. Put the rest of the indoor team to work preparing salads, sauces and other accompaniments, all the time drinking beer.
5. Occasionally pop your head out to pass the barbecuer a fresh beer and words of encouragement, reminding them that this is all for a good cause.
6. When the steaming food is finally brought in, give the nominated barbecuer a big hug to warm them up, then hand them another beer.
7. Enjoy your food!
8. Head out soon after and place something heavy on the BBQ so your neighbour doesn't find the cover in their garden after the next storm.

Liquorice

While *lakkrís* – liquorice – has a cult-like following across the Nordic region, no country has taken its love of the stuff quite as far as Iceland. A massive 75 per cent of Icelandic sweets contain it, often in unusual combinations such as chocolate and caramel-covered liquorice, marzipan-filled liquorice straws and liquorice-coated raisins. Add to that liquorice-flavoured alcohol, liquorice ice cream and thick, black liquorice sauces – you name it, Icelanders will probably put liquorice in it.

Liquorice became popular in the nineteenth century, when it was mainly sold in pharmacies as a cough medicine. Iceland's independence in 1944 brought with it a host of import restrictions, with successive governments trying to keep the exchange rate under control. Restrictions were mainly placed on goods that were considered as non-essential – which unfortunately included most sweets. This meant that everything sweet had to be produced locally, and the already popular and cheap liquorice became a key ingredient to be used in inventive ways. Today, Icelanders have easy access to Mars bars and M&Ms, but still remain loyal to liquorice. Frankly, who could blame them? Coca-Cola just tastes better when sipped through a liquorice straw!

Nammidagur (Sweets Day)

It is sometimes said that Icelanders eat more sweets than any other nation. This may or may not be true, but visitors who venture into Icelandic supermarkets are often taken aback by long aisles bursting with colourful pick 'n' mix sweets.

In an attempt to get this unhealthy habit under some sort of control, many parents took up the concept of *nammidagur* a couple of decades ago. 'Sweets day' is the only time in the week when many Icelandic children are allowed to get their sugar fix, usually on a Saturday. Often, this means a dedicated trip to buy the most desired sweets, with supermarkets giving special Saturday discounts.

However, there are signs that *nammidagur* might be on its way out, with many making the (obvious) point that eating a week's worth of sweets in one day does not equal a healthy lifestyle. Slightly better is the important ritual of the *kósíkvöld*, or 'cosy evening', when, especially during the dark winter months, families sit down together with a bowl of sweets, popcorn or ice cream to watch something good on TV.

Ísbíltúr (Ice-Cream Car Trip)

You might be surprised to see Icelanders queueing up outside an *ísbúð*, or ice-cream shop, on a cold, freezing Monday night in winter. Yet there is nothing unusual about this. Eating *ís* (ice cream) is one of Iceland's favourite pastimes, done all year round and in all weathers. This isn't why the country is called 'Iceland', but it might have something to do with it having a relatively high obesity rate, according to various surveys.

The *ísbíltúr* is a well-known (perhaps even a cultural) phenomenon in Iceland. It consists of going for a drive with the sole intention of going to the ice-cream shop. It is something families do on a Sunday, or a couple might do on a date.

Whether it's cream or milk-based, yoghurt or vegan, ice-cream shops make sure all Icelanders can enjoy their favourite comfort food in lots of different flavours. It can be served in a cone, with a traditional wafer or waffle, or in a box. There are also different dips to choose from (the luxury one, a mixture of chocolate and caramel, is most popular, but there is also dark or white chocolate, caramel, liquorice, and so on), plus condiments (coconut, nuts, more liquorice, Rice Krispies, sweets, etc.). Children might decide on a *trúðaís*, an ice cream served in a cone with the dip and sweets used to create the face of a clown.

The *bragðarefur*, literally translated as 'flavour fox', but also means 'a trickster' could very well be Iceland's best invention. This novelty was first introduced in 1985 by two creative friends who ran an ice-cream shop from a large flower shop inside a greenhouse. Among the things they added to their ice cream was frozen Coca-Cola and bits of Prins Póló chocolate (a Polish chocolate wafer bar that is beloved by Icelanders) – a flavour combination that was hugely popular in the latter half of the twentieth century.

The *bragðarefur* caught on quickly, and you can now ask for it in any ice-cream shop. You can use any sweets and flavours that you like, cake dough, fresh fruit or nuts, the possibilities are endless. It's all mixed in a food processor and is a bit like a personalised McFlurry on steroids, so if you get the chance, do indulge. Our only word of warning is that jelly sweets tend to be hard on the teeth when mixed with ice cream!

Brynjuís in the northern town of Akureyri is one of Iceland's oldest ice-cream shops, and some people say they only eat the stuff when they are there. They've now opened up a new branch in Kópavogur too, in the capital area. Valdís is another popular ice-cream shop in Reykjavík, which opened by the harbour quite recently.

Hnallþóra and Coffee

If you are ever lucky enough to be invited to an Icelandic birthday party or, better yet, a teenager's confirmation party (see page 177), then you are likely to encounter a table swelling with cakes – some of them bigger, with more cream, meringue, berries and chocolate than the others. These are called *hnallþóra*. This isn't, as the name may suggest, a Viking concept (the early settlers didn't spend much time preparing cake buffets), but is named after a character in Halldór Laxness's 1968 novel *Under the Glacier* (*Kristnihald undir Jökli*), who spends most of the book almost force-feeding the male protagonist with her ludicrously over-the-top cakes. The character caught people's imaginations so much that the word *hnallþóra* quickly entered the Icelandic language and has been used ever since to describe this elaborate style of layered cake.

A slice of cake has to be accompanied by a cup of coffee, and Icelanders are huge consumers of the bean (per capita, they often come out as the third-highest in the world). Coffee obviously helps to keep you warm on a cold day, but also serves to keep you awake when the sun barely rises above the horizon in winter.

After centuries of drinking pretty bad coffee in large quantities, Icelanders have started to take the quality of their brew more seriously in recent decades, with shops selling gourmet coffee beans from around the world, and grinders and enormous espresso machines popping up in kitchens everywhere. There's an impressive selection of great cafés all around the country. Check out Mokka in Reykjavík – opened in 1958, it's Iceland's oldest café and artist hangout, with its original furniture still in use. Kaktus Espressobar, also in downtown Reykjavík, serves great Italian coffee and, as the name indicates, plants in pots. In Akureyri, Kaffi Ilmur is a cosy place overlooking the town's main shopping street. In Ísafjörður in the Westfjords, Heimabyggð has great coffee, cakes and food. Meanwhile in Hellnar, a village on the Snæfellsnes peninsula, Fjöruhúsið is a small café hidden down by the water and only open in summer, serving coffee and stunning views.

How To Impress With Your Very Own *Hnallþóra*

Size matters. The cake needs to be at least three tiers high, ideally with a mix of layers, including chocolate or vanilla sponge and, most importantly, at least one meringue layer.

A lot of whipped cream. A typical recipe will have up to a litre of whipped cream in between the layers, and this is where people get really creative. The cream can be flavoured (with chocolate or caramel, for example), but it is also commonly mixed with different types of chopped-up sweets, nuts, berries and fruit, either fresh or from a can. *Þristur*, a chocolate bar with liquorice and caramel, is a popular choice.

Final touches. Don't hold back – pile on more whipped cream and all of your favourite sweet things. Anything goes. The whole thing is then drizzled with a sauce, usually chocolate, caramel or (you guessed it) liquorice.

Skál! (Cheers!)

With a large number of microbreweries producing award-winning craft beer across the country, it may come as a shock to discover that beer was illegal in Iceland until 1989. In 1915 a prohibition law banned the sale of all alcohol. It gradually softened to allow wine (at first only from Spain and Portugal, who had threatened to stop buying Icelandic salted cod) and then stronger spirits, but for decades beer remained off-limits. Some say the reasons for this were patriotic, with Icelanders associating beer with Denmark, their former colonial masters, while others believe that the main reason was a fear that cheap beer would lead to a rise in alcohol abuse.

A locally produced drink, which was popular during the semi-prohibition years, is Brennivín. Created in 1935, the authorities demanded it was sold with a plain black label on the bottle to make it less appealing to the consumer. This earned it the nickname 'Black Death'. A strong, clear spirit made of potatoes and spiced with cumin, Brennivín (which literally translates as 'burning wine', so you get some idea of its effect) is often drunk in a shot, straight out of the freezer. In recent years, it has also started to be used in cocktails, and you might be able to find Brennivín in high-end cocktail bars abroad.

Icelanders today have access to a wide range of alcoholic beverages, but restrictions continue. You can only buy booze in a state-run liquor shop called Vínbúðin, of which there are a total of 52 stores in the whole country. Despite the recent rebranding of Vínbúðin shops to make the shopping experience more pleasant and focused on the appreciation of wine, the old nickname 'Ríkið' ('The State') has been hard to shake off.

Since the beer ban was lifted, overall consumption of alcohol has gradually increased. However, Icelanders still generally drink less than their European neighbours and there is an unusually high percentage of abstinence. Interestingly, the overall rise in consumption has also been accompanied by a move away from the culture of weekend binge-drinking towards a tamer approach, focused on quality rather than quantity. This is evidenced by the excellent local breweries you can find around the country. Ölvisholt brewery in Selfoss and Kaldi brewery in Dalvík, close to the Arctic Circle, both open to the public, are well worth a stop. At Kaldi, you can actually bathe in beer.

Skyr

After fish, the Icelandic product you are most likely to come across in your local supermarket at home is *skyr*.

Resembling yoghurt, but technically a cheese, *skyr* has been a staple food in Iceland for over a thousand years. It's mentioned in the sagas as food served at parties, even used in a food fight in one scene of *The Saga of Grettir the Strong*, and traces of *skyr* have been found during archaeological excavations of medieval farms.

Skyr is made from cow's milk that has had its cream removed. The skimmed milk is then warmed and live cultures of bacteria from a previous batch are added. Once the product has thickened, it is strained to remove the whey. The result is dense and creamy, high in protein and very low in fat and sugar. *Skyr* is therefore a pretty guilt-free snack, and works well on its own, or mixed with berries, seeds, nuts and granola. It is often served as a dessert with full cream and blueberries. It can also be a unique ingredient for a '*skyr* cake' (think cheesecake) or even for a tiramisù-inspired '*skyramisù*'.

Due to its recent marketing as a superfood, *skyr* has become a fast-growing export, with Icelandic producers even setting up production overseas to meet demand. Beware of imitations though – numerous non-Icelandic brands have popped up with little or no connection to the original Viking tried-and-tested recipe. The words 'Icelandic style' on the packaging are usually a giveaway!

Five a Day

Iceland's short summers are not exactly suited to growing vegetables. For most of the one thousand years after the first settlement, the population survived almost exclusively (and, at times, only just) on animal products. For centuries, there was even an arguable reluctance among Icelandic farmers to waste their precious grazing fields on growing crops. The cultivation of potatoes and other root vegetables only really took off in the early nineteenth century and other cold-weather vegetables such as cabbage didn't feature heavily in traditional cooking.

If vegetables were hard to come by, then fruit was an exotic delicacy, even well into the twentieth century. As recently as the 1960s, apples were considered a special Christmas treat. There was even a period in the 1930s when you could only get oranges if you had a doctor's prescription for them.

Despite no vegetables being native to Iceland, in the past, most people would have had some late-summer access to fruit in the form of wild blueberries and bilberries, as well as mushrooms. With the greater availability of sugar in the nineteenth century, berries and rhubarb started to be used for jams, juices and compotes.

Icelanders still consume less fruit and vegetables than other Europeans, and tourists have often complained about the rather sad-looking produce that has travelled the globe before arriving in an Icelandic supermarket. However, the last few decades have seen a real vegetable revolution. Thanks to geothermal energy providing heat and light to greenhouses, vegetables can be grown all year round, and the bulk of Iceland's tomatoes, cucumbers, peppers and lettuce available to buy is now produced locally. Vegetarianism and veganism are also on the rise, and Iceland can even claim to have the greatest number of vegetarian restaurants in Europe (per capita, of course).

LIFE OUTDOORS

No Such Thing as Bad Weather

Living just below the Arctic Circle teaches you a thing or two about how to live with the natural elements. From a very young age we go out in all weathers. Newborns sleep outside in their prams all year round and wake up happy with red cheeks after being swayed by the cold wind. At kindergarten, children play outside for a large part of the day, eating snow and black volcanic sand. Kids normally walk to school unsupervised in almost any weather from a very young age (see page 172). An important life lesson we all learn is how to walk on ice (insider tip: mimic a penguin). We also discover how you need to walk head-on into wind and that sometimes you need to turn sideways to gasp for air. All Icelanders know that there is no such thing as bad weather – only inappropriate clothing! With that in mind, keep an eye out for brands such as 66°North (keeping cool Icelanders warm since 1926), Cintamani, ZO•ON and Icewear.

Hiking in the Great Outdoors

Most Icelanders enjoy nature (when properly dressed), although we are arguably not as fanatical about it as some of our Nordic neighbours. We are not Norway, where children seem to be born with skis on their feet. That said, hiking in the mountains is a very popular activity.

There are several travel clubs or associations to help you find your way, such as Ferðafélag Íslands (FÍ), known in English as the Iceland Touring Association, and Útivist. They organise a variety of tours for members and non-members alike and run mountain huts across the country, where you can find basic, essential accommodation.

There are several trails that are very popular. Fimmvörðuháls ('the five cairns ridge') is a popular trek that goes from Skógar on the south coast to Þórsmörk, a stunning area surrounded by glaciers. The trek goes over the ridge between two glaciers – Mýrdalsjökull and Eyjafjallajökull (internationally infamous for the ash cloud the volcano underneath produced in 2010). The trek takes about nine hours. From Þórsmörk lies another path, Laugavegur (literally 'pool way', incidentally also the name of the main shopping street in Reykjavík). This trail goes to Landmannalaugar, a place of incredible beauty at the end of an obsidian lava flow in an area of multicoloured rhyolite mountains and steamy geothermal pools. There is a mountain hut accommodation run by FÍ, next to a natural pool that is an absolute must-visit. The Laugavegur trek is about 55 kilometres (34 miles) long and is normally completed from Landmannalaugar in four days, staying in different huts along the way. On this route, several rivers must be crossed on foot.

Wonderful hiking can be found around the country. For hikes in the winter, it is important never to go on your own, and to bring crampons and even an ice axe and a helmet, depending on where you are going. Also remember to check the weather forecast before you head off and make sure you tell someone your plans.

Always On Call

Icelandic nature is breathtakingly beautiful – but can be equally dangerous. With the risk of extreme weather and avalanches amongst the many dangers to be found in the wilderness, locals and tourists alike sometimes find themselves in trouble. Who ya gonna call? The Rescue Team!

Icelandic rescue teams are made up of volunteers who specialise in rescue efforts on land, sea and in the mountains. These groups are comprised of people trained to be ready to assist in extreme circumstances and to leave their families or jobs at any time of the day or night, all year round, without any renumeration except the pleasure of being able to help. These people really are our everyday heroes.

The variety of missions covered by the search and rescue teams in Iceland is also unique. Helping a fishing boat in difficulty, finding a lost tourist on a mountain, rescuing an injured hiker or nailing down loose roofs during a storm are all examples of the work they do. We do have a Coast Guard, but in the absence of an army in Iceland, rescue teams are always present during the country's hour of need.

A total of 93 teams and 37 accident-prevention divisions are scattered across the country, with almost 18,000 members, about 4,500 of which are always on call. Each year, rescue teams get called out on an average of 1,200 occasions.

While rescue teams are extremely well-trained and equipped, they receive very little state funding and rescue workers even pay for their own personal equipment. The rescue teams are mostly financed by the general public, particularly through the selling of fireworks at New Year's Eve (see page 204).

The oldest rescue teams were formed almost a hundred years ago and focused at first on safety at sea. Their aim was to no longer accept the old saying that 'the sea gives, the sea takes' (see page 15). Slysavarnarfélagið Landsbjörg, the Icelandic Association for Search and Rescue (ICE-SAR), is the umbrella organisation for the teams, operating 13 rescue vessels around the country and also running intensive training courses on maritime safety and survival for seafarers.

ICE-SAR operates www.safetravel.is, which provides a wealth of vital information about safety while travelling in Iceland, including how to drive, outdoor activities, weather and road conditions. You can also submit a travel plan, with your expected time of return. If you fail to mark your trip as completed, an alarm will be raised. You can also download the 112 app that allows you to call for assistance in case of need, providing rescue teams with your location through your phone.

Outdoor Sport

Skiing

Icelanders mostly ski in winter, in and around ski resorts. Cross-country skiing can also be done on the glaciers in the summertime, with the best conditions being in spring (but of course *only* if you are experienced or go with a guide). It might sound strange, but it's not always a given that you can go skiing at an Icelandic ski resort in winter, especially the ones in the south. Icelandic mountains are relatively low compared to, say, the Alps, and often there simply isn't enough snow – especially in recent years as global warming takes effect. Ski enthusiasts from Reykjavík often head north to Akureyri or Ísafjörður for the weekend. Some companies also offer heli-skiing – taking people up to the tops of mountains in helicopters so they can ski all the way to the bottom before flying up again.

Climbing

Ice climbing on glaciers is quite popular, at least among the most outdoorsy types. It is quite easy to reach crevasses at glacier tongues, where glaciers descend down from the ice cap. Ice climbing can also be done on frozen waterfalls, when the conditions are right. Of course, all activities like these should be done with a local guide.

Rock climbing can also be done in various places in Iceland. For example, at Hnappavellir, on the south-east coast, where there are many different bolted lines, trad routes and boulder problems. There are very limited facilities, so the area is intended for climbers only.

Cycling

Over the last few years, cycling as a sport, both racing and in the mountains, has become increasingly popular. Cycling is a great way to experience Iceland, but saying that conditions can be difficult is putting it mildly. Wind can cause major problems and some roads in the highlands are not great, so good suspension is vital. Iceland's national ring road is also narrow, so there's not much space to cycle safely next to the motor traffic, as there are no specific bike lanes. The same advice applies to cycling as to every other outdoor activity in Iceland: it is important to dress well, check the weather forecast and tell someone where you're going before heading off.

Kayaking

Along with other ocean-based sports, kayaking has become popular over the last few years in Iceland. The best conditions for kayaking are often in the evening or night, when the wind usually drops. In the summer months, the time of day doesn't matter, as we have daylight around the clock. When the ocean is completely still, you are rewarded with a perfect view into the clear water – and you might encounter seals or even a minke whale.

Running

Iceland is great for running. Reykjavík has plenty of paths and nature on its doorstep, with air pollution levels so low that you can safely run for hours without worry. When the ground is slippery in winter, you can put spikes on your trainers just to be on the safe side; in summer, running in the endless daylight is exhilarating. The Midnight Sun Run takes place in Reykjavík late at night, around the time of the summer solstice in June. There are several other organised runs, with the biggest being the Reykjavík Marathon. Runners can choose between various distances and there is a fun run for kids as well. If trail running is more your thing, the Laugavegur Ultra Marathon is a 55-kilometer (34-mile) race across a nature reserve in the southern highlands – also a popular hiking route (see page 125) – that takes place in July. The course involves crossing cold rivers with possible rain, wind and even snow, so not one for the fainthearted.

Golfing Under the Midnight Sun

Golf courses in Iceland are generally located amid beautiful and dramatic scenery, such as on the coast or next to a lava field. Many courses stay open 24/7 during the summer and the unique experience of a round of golf at midnight is a definite draw. The Arctic Open Golf Championship in Akureyri offers this in a competitive setting and participants come from all over the world.

LIFE OUTDOORS

Tölt-ing on Your Icelandic Horse

The first settlers in Iceland brought horses from Norway and the species has been isolated here ever since, making it one of the purest pedigrees in the world. The settlers are said to have carefully selected the horses they brought with them, so the Icelandic horse comes from good stock.

The breed is known for being very good-tempered, strong and sturdy. It is smaller than most horses (but don't ever consider referring to it as a pony). An important feature of the Icelandic horse is that it has two unique gaits – ways of moving – not shared by other breeds. These are *tölt* and *skeið*. *Tölt* is a very smooth way of riding – to demonstrate this, the rider sometimes holds a glass of beer to show that almost none of it gets spilled. *Skeið* is super-fast, sometimes described as 'fifth gear' or 'flying pace', but this gait is only used for short distances.

The isolation of the Icelandic horse means it is vulnerable to diseases that are not prevalent in Iceland. Riders must therefore disinfect all gear that has been in contact with horses abroad before using it in Iceland. It is also forbidden to import horses to Iceland, and if an Icelandic horse leaves the country, it can never return. That is the fate of the horses that travel to the overseas World Championships for Icelandic Horses. The qualities of the Icelandic horse have made it quite a popular breed and each year around 1,500 horses are exported from Iceland, mostly to Germany. In Iceland, *Landsmót* (the National Icelandic Horse Competition) is held every other summer, featuring all the best horses.

Fishing and Hunting

Icelanders like to fetch their own food from nature. Salmon and trout fishing are very popular in the summer, with the season running from April until October. Access to some rivers is very expensive indeed, running to hundreds of thousands of *krónur* per day. Fishing in the priciest areas is not something the average Icelander can enjoy, but royalty, rock stars and billionaires frequently come to Iceland to fish, drawn by the diversity of the rivers, the beautiful landscapes and the wild Atlantic salmon. People can stay in fishing lodges, where an excellent cook will prepare fabulous meals. There are plenty of less expensive salmon rivers however, and freshwater fishing is accessible too.

Fishing is a popular sport in many families and children learn to use a fishing rod early on. As adults, many Icelanders belong to one or even multiple fishing groups, often with their friends, and go fishing as part of a long weekend at least once a year. Women are becoming more active within the fishing community, but fishing groups are more common among men – perhaps they are the male version of a sewing club (see page 152).

Away from rivers, ptarmigan (a type of game bird), geese and reindeer are hunted in Iceland, along with some seabirds. Reindeer were imported to Iceland in the eighteenth century and are only found in the eastern highlands. A limited number can be hunted every year and, as food is scarce during winter, it is necessary to cull some to ensure the survival of the herd. As the number of ptarmigan has fallen in recent years, hunting is only allowed for private consumption and the season is very short. At the time of writing, it was permitted mainly in November and only on specific days of the week. For families who know hunters, ptarmigan, reindeer or goose are all options for the Christmas table.

Camping

Icelanders love to spend their nights under canvas. There is something magical about a summer night spent lying in a tent under the midnight sun and listening to nothing more than a multitude of birds chirping away. You might also hear the occasional bleat of a sheep.

Hardcore campers carry everything on their backs, pitch a tent for the night, cook on their primus stove and set off early next morning to continue their trek. These tend to be tourists. Icelandic campers tend to prefer something a little more sedate. For many, camping is a lifestyle, so they will bring huge tents, trailers or camper vans loaded up with every luxury item they might possibly need. They will even bring a TV set, loads of boardgames and a barbecue. Many Icelanders associate camping with partying, especially during the festival weekend in late summer (see page 217).

The Pool – A Bare Necessity of Life

If you are planning a trip to Iceland, don't forget to pack your swimsuit. Without doubt, Icelanders' favourite activity is going to the swimming pool. One major benefit of the abundance of geothermal energy is that an outdoor, heated pool is never far away. Bathing outside in hot water is an old tradition and it's even mentioned in the sagas.

Icelanders consider access to a swimming pool as a major necessity in life. There are more than 100 pools around Iceland that are open to the public, 17 of them located in Reykjavík. At www.sundlaugar.is there is detailed information about all of them, often with pictures showing the pool and other amenities such as hot and cold tubs, saunas and waterslides.

Outdoor pools are hugely popular all year round and in any weather. In fact, going to the pool is particularly nice when the weather is gloomy. You get a dose of healthy fresh air and can marinate in the hot water as the snowflakes fall on you. When your shoulders and head get cold, just go under for a few seconds to warm up.

Going to the pool isn't always about swimming. Some people go at the same time each day to sit in the hot tubs and talk about politics and current

affairs with the other regular pool-goers. It's not unusual to have a government minister having a soak with a poet, a schoolteacher, a plumber and a cook, all in lively debate. Many people just go to the pool to lie in the hot tub while their kids enjoy the waterslides. A lot of pools are open until quite late in the evening and if you go just after dinner you'll notice some people putting their pyjamas on when leaving, particularly the children. We can assure you that kids fall asleep very quickly after an evening in the pool.

Off to the Showers Everyone!

Icelandic pools are very clean because new water is pumped through them continuously. As not as much chlorine is used compared to pools in many other countries, everyone is required to wash thoroughly beforehand in separate changing rooms for women and men. It doesn't matter if you've just had a shower at home – before putting on your swimsuit, you must shower naked using soap immediately before entering the pool. Not doing so is frowned upon deeply by Icelanders. Nobody cares about the shape or size of your body: but if you don't shower, you'll get a nasty stare and someone might even tell you off.

Growing up with communal showering, Icelanders learn early on that the human body comes in all sizes, shapes and forms, and that skin becomes wrinkled and breasts and bottoms sag with age. We see everyone naked – large and small people, pregnant women, people with scars and disabilities. As a result, in Iceland we perhaps have a more natural attitude towards the human body – we are used to seeing the real thing all the time, not just an Instagram version of perfection.

How To Blend In at an Icelandic Swimming Pool
- Remove your shoes before entering the changing room and leave them outside.
- Take off all your clothes and put them in the locker. Don't put your swimming gear on yet. Take your towel, shampoo and swimsuit to the showers, along with your goggles if you're planning to go for a serious swim.
- Leave your towel in the designated area.
- Shower naked and use the provided soap freely. You'll see a sign in many languages showing you that you are required to wash your head, armpits, genitals and feet. Do so.
- When done, put on your swimsuit and either go for a swim or head to the hot tub.
- When you reach the hot tub, say '*Góðan daginn*' ('good day') to anyone else present when you find a spot.
- If there is a heated debate going on, nod your head and utter the occasional '*þetta reddast*' and '*jæja*' and see what happens (see pages 48 and 63).
- When leaving, shower again. We don't really care if you use soap on your way out. However, under no circumstances should you try to shave any body hair in the showers.
- Dry off in the designated drying area, as we don't like puddles of water where we are putting our clothes back on.
- We recommend drying your hair with the hairdryers provided, particularly if the weather outside is cold.
- Icelanders often end a trip to the pool by eating a *pulsa* (see page 103) or an ice cream (perhaps a 'flavour fox' (see page 110) if you want to be a bit extravagant). You'll usually find hot-dog stands and ice-cream shops in the vicinity of pools.

LIFE INSIDE

Window Weather

Icelanders are tough people who will head out in all weathers for work and leisure (as the 'Life Outdoors' chapter shows). However, for obvious reasons, we do spend a lot of our time indoors. Icelandic homes are built to withstand earthquakes, are heated with piping-hot geothermal water (including our driveways), are powered by completely renewable energy, and benefit from some of the fastest internet speeds in the world – so it's not surprising that we might prefer to curl up under a blanket to enjoy watching the ever-changing weather through a window.

Heima Er Best (Home Is the Best Place To Be)

While for Icelanders the home is a refuge from the often unhospitable outside world, it is by no means a closed-off, insular space. Icelandic homes tend to be open – often literally, with front doors left unlocked to let children come and go. There are no shutters on windows, and curtains tend to be drawn right back to let in all the light. Dropping by at someone's house unannounced is not considered rude and Icelanders will invite friends and family over for coffee or dinner both frequently and often at short notice. Considering all the traffic in and out of a typical home, it is important to follow one rule: always take your shoes off before you enter. You can drop by uninvited, but if you don't remove your shoes first, you're in trouble.

Icelanders are houseproud and many of us put a lot of effort into making our homes look good. Interior design and home improvement are popular hobbies. Many television programmes and magazines are devoted to design, and Instagram is full of photos of the trendiest homes. With the outside of Icelandic homes often battered by storms and sea salt, and perfectly manicured lawns and trimmed hedges rather rare, overseas visitors are often surprised to find a stylish interior full of the latest carefully selected design pieces once they step foot inside.

10 Steps to Making Your Home Look and Feel Icelandic

Step 1: Pretend someone else is paying your bills and turn up the radiators until your home feels very toasty. Then open all the windows to bring in the fresh air and switch on all the lights.

Step 2: Get yourself a view, ideally of the ocean, plus some majestic mountains.

Step 3: Don't have lots of bathrooms but do install a hot tub in your garden.

Step 4: Make sure the kitchen is big enough for a 'kitchen party', or at least a *trúnó* (an intense conversation with friends) (see page 79).

Step 5: Paint your home in light colours (possibly do a couple of walls in grey) and furnish with minimalist mid-century Scandinavian furniture, plus a few pieces from IKEA.

Step 6: Add cosy finishing touches to the minimalism, such as woollen or sheepskin rugs, warm throws and cushions. Light lots of candles.

Step 7: Mix new and old. Hang on to your grandfather's old armchair and the family silver.

Step 8: Hang original art on your walls, ideally by an artist you know personally, or paintings that have been in the family for a while.

Step 9: Fill your shelves with books, but also get yourself a huge TV.

Step 10: Keep updating and follow the latest trends (an Icelandic time-traveller could tell, with some precision, what year it is just from the make of vase displayed on a dining table).

One final, but important, detail: get yourself at least one Moomin mug. They are from Finland, but we love them!

The Home From Home

Drive an hour away from Reykjavík and you'll soon see small wooden houses, often with colourful roofs, dotted around south-facing slopes. Often these houses are nestled together so that they almost look like villages, but they are not. These are our summer houses. Many city-dwellers escape to their summer houses whenever they have time off – especially when the weekend forecast is sunny.

From the sheer number of houses, you might think that every family has its own, but this is far from the case. Many summer houses are owned and used by extended families or groups of friends, and most workers' unions and associations own summer houses that are rented out cheaply, by the week, to their members, allowing most Icelandic families regular access to one.

The summer-house culture is a recent phenomenon, only dating back to the post-war period when Icelanders made the great move from the country to towns and more people started to receive paid summer leave, so most of the houses you will see are quite new. The style is similar to that found across the Nordic countries: simple wooden structures with high gables and large windows (unlike regular Icelandic homes, which are almost always made of concrete). Some of the more recent houses are completely prefabricated in local workshops, but quite often the building of a summer house is a joint venture, where generations add bits here and there to adapt to the growing size of the family and developing requirements.

Unlike many other countries, where summer houses tend to be not much more than basic huts, Icelandic summer houses are usually fully furnished and equipped as normal homes, with running water, electricity and wi-fi as standard. Any decent house will naturally also have a hot tub installed on the deck, usually placed strategically on the sunny and least windy side of the house. On the inside, most summer houses are simple, with warmth and cosiness prioritised over any attempt to keep up with the latest design trends.

Summer houses could feature in the 'Life Outdoors' chapter of this book, as Icelanders use them as a base for hiking, sightseeing and sport. However, going to the summer house with family or a group of friends is often mainly about spending time relaxing at the house itself – lying in the hot tub, preparing food on the barbecue, playing boardgames, reading, or simply falling asleep to the sound of birch trees rustling in the wind.

Close-knit Sewing Clubs

The vast majority of Icelandic women belong to a *saumaklúbbur*, or 'sewing club', that meets regularly. Women under 30 might not call their group a 'sewing club', but the concept remains the same.

Sewing clubs started to take off in the early twentieth century, when Icelanders moved to towns in large numbers. The clubs often provided an opportunity for women to maintain links with friends from their home regions, who were also new in town, and therefore provided an important social network. As women didn't think they could be seen spending an evening every month idly having fun, they would bring needlework or knitting to work on while chatting. The 1970s saw a backlash against the concept, with many complaining that it was outdated and that women shouldn't have to use such a pretext to meet. However, despite important changes in the role of women inside and outside the home over the past few decades, the sewing club has survived.

Most clubs are made up of a small group of women who have been friends since childhood and who, as adults, often have very little in common, other than the sewing club they belong to. A typical club can easily represent a wide cross-section of society, with a company CEO meeting up with her 'girls' who include a teacher, a secretary, a farmer and an opera singer, all because they happened to be in the same class at school when they were 10 years old. Often, the lifelong friendship bonds between club members are very strong, providing women with an important source of practical and emotional support.

At a typical sewing club meeting, there is usually very little sewing involved, if any at all. Some clubs are sporty and will go running or hiking, or they will go to someone's summer house for the weekend. Most often, women will meet up in the home of one of the members for dinner or nibbles, with the host often testing new recipes on her friends. There will be lots of talking, laughing and problem-solving until late, when they all head home reinvigorated and ready to tackle their (often vastly different) everyday lives.

Knitting

Icelanders are keen knitters. Knitting was introduced in the sixteenth century and, well into the nineteenth century, woollen goods were an important export for the country. Knitting was one of the main sources of income for many families and it was a key activity, especially during the long winter months, that all family members contributed to: men, women and children.

Icelanders no longer knit to stay alive, but it is still a popular hobby, with techniques handed down through generations and every child learning how to knit at school. When an Icelandic baby is born, it will almost certainly receive something hand-knitted and even the clumsiest of parents-to-be will feel under some social pressure to at least knit a blanket for their baby. Often, a big effort is made to knit a *heimferðarsett* ('homecoming set') for a newborn – a matching set of clothes that the child will be dressed in for its first journey home from the hospital. It usually consists of an all-in-one suit (or a sweater and trousers), a hat, mittens and socks.

It is notable that the popularity of knitting seems to increase in times of crisis. Following the 2008 financial crisis, there was an enormous surge in the sale of yarn and a lot of knitting groups popped up online. Apparently, knitting as a response to crisis makes sense. Its calming effects have been likened to yoga and meditation, but knitting also yields a very practical result: a new item of clothing.

The *Lopapeysa*

One of the most well-known symbols of Iceland is the *lopapeysa*, a sweater made of strong, warm and water-resistant wool from Icelandic sheep (*lopi*), with a distinctive round pattern (or 'yoke') around the neck. Every Icelander owns one (they are so sturdy that one sweater should last you a lifetime) and tens of thousands are sold to tourists visiting the country every year.

However, the *lopapeysa* has been described as an example of an 'invented tradition', as the method and design only date back to the mid-twentieth century, when the arrival of the circular knitting needle made the pattern easy to produce. The origin of the design is disputed, with some saying it was borrowed from Greenland, where the traditional dress has a beaded collar that looks similar to the *lopapeysa* yoke. Regardless of its exact origin, the sweater has become an inseparable part of Iceland's cultural identity.

It has had a huge resurgence in popularity in recent years, perhaps due to its association with a simpler, back-to-nature lifestyle, as well as the growth in tourism. Ironically, this yearning for simplicity has meant that Icelandic knitters haven't been able to keep up with demand, and many sweaters found in shops are hand-knitted in China. Wool from Icelandic sheep is shipped off to be made into sweaters by Chinese knitters, then shipped back again and labelled as 'handmade from Icelandic wool'. To be sure you have an authentic locally made *lopapeysa*, keep an eye out for the 'Handknitting Association of Iceland' label.

Sing!

Chances are that if you join any kind of celebration in Iceland, at some point, someone will burst into song and very quickly the whole group will join in, with everyone knowing the words.

It is estimated that there are around 300 amateur choirs in Iceland, comprising around 10,000 active members. These choirs come in all shapes and sizes: church choirs, gospel choirs, school choirs, workplace choirs, choirs linked to associations, LGBTQIA+ choirs, regional and neighbourhood choirs, senior citizens' choirs, all-women and all-men choirs, there's even an 'ugly' choir, and a choir made up of the regulars at Kaffibarinn (a popular bar in Reykjavik). The choirs also cover the whole spectrum of musical genres, from opera and classical to religious, folk, pop and rock.

The Icelandic urge to sing together is so strong that wherever Icelanders settle in any reasonable numbers abroad (i.e. more than 20), they tend to form a choir. They don't even have to settle; in the Canary Islands, where a community of mostly retired Icelanders spends the coldest winter months keeping warm in the sun, over 200 people meet each week to sing popular Icelandic songs.

A word of warning: while Icelanders love to sing, never ask anyone to sing Iceland's national anthem for you. You'll either embarrass them or they'll sing something completely different, pretending it's the national anthem. The actual anthem (called *Lofsöngur*) is notoriously long and hard to perform. Unless you're Céline Dion, it really requires a full choir to span the extreme vocal range. Every few years there are proposals to replace the anthem with something easier to sing, with most people agreeing that *something* should be done – but so far there's been no agreement as to what should replace it.

Community Theatre

Community theatre has a long and unusually dynamic history in Iceland. Records show that in the late nineteenth century, when the total number of citizens was only around 70,000, there were active theatre groups in around fifty villages and hamlets, keeping the population entertained.

Even with the wide range of culture and entertainment on offer in Iceland today, amateur theatre is still going strong (especially outside the capital), with around 80 plays and musicals staged each year.

Local productions are often extremely ambitious. In 2019, the theatre group in Húnaþing vestra, a tiny, mainly rural municipality in the north-west of Iceland, with a population of just 1,200 people, put on a huge production of the musical *Hair* with almost 50 local actors, singers and musicians. According to the group's records, they sold 1,000 tickets! To top it all off, the production was chosen as the best of the year at the annual Amateur Theatre Awards, the reward being an invitation to bring the show to the main stage of the National Theatre in Reykjavík.

Indoor Sport

Indoor sporting activities are hugely popular in Iceland, which is unsurprising for a country where the weather can quickly put paid to any planned activities outside – and it has led to the rest of the world taking notice.

Football

Yes, football isn't technically an indoor sport – but many credit the incredible success of Icelandic football in recent years to the decision to bring it indoors. In the early 2000s, football clubs and local authorities got together to build covered pitches all around the country. They are heated, well-equipped, open to everyone and staffed with professional coaches for all ages. In the darkest winter months, not having to start a training session by shovelling snow off the grass can make a world of difference.

Handball

Long before Icelanders became good at football, there was handball. For decades, Iceland's teams have been among the top-ranked in the world, winning the silver medal at the 2008 Olympics and a bronze medal in the 2010 European Men's Handball Championship. Handball is quite possibly Iceland's national sport and almost 8,000 people actively play it.

CrossFit

CrossFit is high-intensity interval training that combines weightlifting, running, rowing and other activities. It's known internationally, but in Iceland it is particularly popular, with thousands of people sweating it out every week. Icelandic women are extremely good at CrossFit and have dominated it at global levels in recent years. The 'Fittest on Earth' title at the CrossFit Games has gone to an Icelandic woman four times. In their honour, CrossFit has created a special workout routine called *dóttir* (daughter).

Chess

It's debatable whether chess is a sport or an artform, but for decades it was the only competitive activity that Icelanders excelled at internationally. In its heyday in the 1970s and 80s, Icelandic chess players did very well at international championships and were celebrated as national heroes. In 1972, a now-legendary World Chess Championship final between Bobby Fischer and Boris Spassky was held in Reykjavík. At the height of the Cold War, this clash between the USA and the USSR was a major news event and the eyes of the world were on Iceland for the first time. The whole country went into a chess frenzy.

There is rather less excitement about chess today and it is no longer shown on primetime television, but there are still dozens of chess clubs around the country for all ages and we still have more Grandmasters than any other country (per capita, of course).

Gaming

A 2019 study showed that two out of three Icelanders play video games regularly, with the proportion of players going up to nearly 100 per cent in younger age groups. These figures are probably quite similar to what you might find in other countries, but in recent years there's been an interesting move towards re-categorising gaming as an organised sport and social activity. The aim is to get gaming out of teenagers' bedrooms and into clubs where they can train, compete and interact with others under the supervision of coaches. Organised gaming clubs have sprung up all around the country under the auspices of local sports clubs, bringing in many young people who have not been drawn to traditional sport.

This list of indoor sports is by no means exhaustive, but it does give you an idea of the sports we're probably most passionate about. Some say the most important exercise of all is reading – in which Icelanders are possibly the world champions.

FAMILY LIFE AND LIFE'S MILESTONES

Birth

Let's start at the beginning. A child born in Iceland is likely to weigh more than 3.5 kilograms (just over 7 pounds 7 ounces) – slightly heavier than the average European newborn. In a typical scenario, a trained midwife (*ljósmóðir*, literally 'mother of light') will attend the delivery, which usually takes place in a hospital or maternity centre, but less than one in five births will be assisted or via C-section. In fact, the mother is unlikely to have much medical intervention throughout the pregnancy, with nature allowed to pretty much take its course. Mother and child will normally spend just one night in hospital if there are no complications, and sometimes they can even return home on the same day as the birth.

The newborn baby will probably not be named right away, with the parents waiting to get to know the child before making a decision. Usually, this period lasts for about three months, but by law can go up to six. Until the naming, the child will simply go by *stúlka* (girl) or *drengur* (boy) in official documents.

The child's parents will likely not be married and are probably less than 30 years old when they have their first baby. Generally, the child will end up with at least one biological sibling, and could very well acquire some half-siblings later on. In Iceland, the concept of the nuclear family with 2.4 children doesn't really apply. For the first year, the child will stay at home with their parents during 12 months of shared parental leave, sleeping outside every day in a pram. Later, the child is looked after by a *dagforeldri* ('day-parent', the Icelandic term for a childminder), then, from about the age of two, attends a preschool, where they will spend the next 4–5 years with minimal supervision, messing about outdoors in all weathers, getting covered in mud and snot. Despite this (or probably because of this), the child is almost guaranteed to survive past the age of five and will have a life expectancy of almost 83 years.

Tracing Your Roots

When two Icelanders meet for the first time, they are very likely to ask *'Hverra manna ertu?'* – 'Who are your people?' As surnames passed through generations don't generally exist in Iceland, this is how we go about locating and categorising a new person, as well as identifying common ancestors.

Concern about the risk of possibly incestuous pairings in a nation with a small population is not at all the reason for the Icelandic obsession with genealogy. People are simply fascinated by how they are connected to one another and want to trace their roots, ideally all the way back to the first settlers. Bookshops and libraries are full of books on the histories of families, and many Icelanders gather regularly at large *ættarmót* (a bit like clan gatherings), where sometimes hundreds of descendants of a given ancestor meet for a weekend of celebration. Icelanders use the terms *frænka* (aunt) and *frændi* (uncle) very generously to refer to anyone even remotely related, with no need for any 'twice-removed' caveats. If you know you are somehow related, you can refer to a person as *frændi* or *frænka*. These words have the same root as 'friend' in English, so they can basically refer to anyone with whom you share kinship. Indeed, *kyn* means 'family' or 'race' in Icelandic.

Impeccable church records, censuses and family archives dating back almost a millennium make all this possible. In recent years, Icelanders have been able to access these genealogical sources online through the *Íslendingabók* (*The Book of Icelanders*), a database created by a biotech company that attempts to record the genealogy of all Icelanders who have ever lived, and is named after the famous twelfth-century history book. Indeed, it is fairly easy for Icelanders to trace themselves to any other Icelander, no matter how far back. The first settlers of Iceland, Ingólfur Arnarson and Hallveig Fróðadóttir, are the direct ancestors of the authors of the book you are now reading, 30 generations back.

Naming Conventions

Unlike in most other western countries, the vast majority of Icelanders do not have family surnames. A person's last name refers to the first name of their father or mother, and not to any family lineage. This is called a patronym (or it could also be a *ma*tronym).

Sons and Daughters

The last name of male Icelanders ends in the suffix *-son* (son) and that of female Icelanders in *-dóttir* (daughter). For example, Iceland's first female president is Vigdís Finnbogadóttir, so her father's first name was Finnbogi, as her last name is 'Finnbogi's daughter'. While the patronym is still most common, the matronym is increasingly used, and some people even use both. Dagur Bergþóruson Eggertsson, the mayor of Reykjavík at the time of writing, is Dagur, son of Bergþóra (his mother) and son of Eggert (his father). In 2019, a new law was passed that also allowed for the use of the non-gendered suffix *-bur* (meaning 'child of').

Family Names

About four per cent of the population does have a family name, usually either adopted before 1925 (when taking a new family name was banned) or if a person has a parent from overseas. One famous Icelander with a pre-1925 name was the author Halldór Laxness. He was born Halldór Guðjónsson, but took the name Laxness in reference to the farm where he grew up. Due to the lack of family names, Icelanders often name their children after someone else in the family, typically the grandparents. Often, there are generations of family members with the same names. In the family of Nína, the co-author of this book, the men have been named Ingimar or Jón for five generations. Her brother is Ingimar Jónsson and her father is Jón Ingimarsson. Nína's paternal grandfather is Ingimar Jónsson, son of Jón Ingimarsson.

Icelandic women obviously do not take their husbands' names, as that simply wouldn't make any sense: a woman can't become the son of her father-in-law. Families will therefore often not have any last name in common, unless there is more than one daughter or son. Icelandic parents traveling abroad with their children frequently find themselves having to explain Icelandic naming practices at length to confused immigration officers and hotel receptionists.

First Names Really Matter in Iceland

When choosing what to call a child, parents have to stick to a list of approved first and middle names. There are over 1,800 female names and 1,700 male names on the list, and each year sees new entries.

If parents want to go for a name that isn't on the list, they have to send a request to the *Mannanafnanefnd* (naming committee). The criterion for the acceptance of names is whether or not they can be incorporated grammatically into the Icelandic language. Recent refusals include Lucifer and Zelda, but also more surprisingly (at least to English speakers) Harriet and Duncan.

There are some interesting cultural implications of Iceland's naming tradition. Icelanders will always refer to each other by their first names. It doesn't matter if you are a police officer, a primary school teacher or the president – people will always address you by your first name. All directories are alphabetised by first name (with the addition of middle names and professions to avoid confusion).

How To Make Your Name Icelandic
Your current name: George Windsor
Step 1: Is your first name on the naming committee's list? You're in luck, George has recently been allowed, but the most common Icelandic spelling is Georg.
Step 2: What are your parents' first names? Do they appear on the list? William is another recent addition and Catherine isn't, but the Icelandic equivalents are there as Vilhjálmur and Katrín.
Step 3: Do you want to go for a patronym or a matronym? Let's go for a matronym for a change.
So, George Windsor becomes Georg Katrínarson.

Icelandic Names

(Yes, These Are Approved by the Committee)

Boys
Bogi: 'Bow'
Dagur: 'Day'
Erlendur: 'Foreign'
Hrafn: 'Raven'
Jökull: 'Glacier'
Oddur: 'Point of a knife'
Ófeigur: 'Immortal'
Skjöldur: 'Shield'
Stormur: 'Storm'
Þorsteinn: 'The rock belonging to the god Thor'
Örn: 'Eagle'
Örvar: 'Arrows'

Girls
Alda: 'Wave'
Birta: 'Brightness'
Fönn: 'Snow'
Gló: 'Spark'
Heiður: 'Honour'
Hekla: A famous Icelandic volcano
Hulda: 'Female elf'
Ilmur: 'Scent'
Ísey: 'Ice island'
Líf: 'Life'
Lóa: 'The golden plover' (see page 213)
Ósk: 'Wish'
Sigurdís: 'Victory goddess'
Snærós: 'Snow rose'
Sóley: 'Buttercup'
Steinbjörg: 'Stone/rock salvation'
Ugla: 'Owl'

Gender-neutral
Auður: 'Wealth'
Blær: 'Breeze'
Eir: 'Copper'
Frost: 'Frost'
Karma: 'Karma'
Júní: 'June'
Júlí: 'July'
Regn: 'Rain'

The Freedom of an Icelandic Childhood

If there is one word that sums up childhood in Iceland, it is 'freedom'. Kids are allowed to play outside on their own from quite a young age (gradually, of course) and roam their neighbourhoods happily.

Primary school starts from the age of six, with each class made up of children born in the same calendar year. Pupils will often stay at the same school until they are 13, then they'll either transfer to another building in the same school or go to a different secondary school. Almost all Icelandic children attend their local school, which is run by the local authorities. In addition to the usual subjects you would expect to be taught at every school, Icelandic kids, regardless of gender, all learn knitting, sewing, textile work, carpentry, cooking and swimming. They have regular swimming lessons between the ages of six and 15 and need to pass a swimming test.

Most children in urban areas live close to their school and from when they're about seven years old they walk in every morning, even in winter. Sometimes it is announced on the radio that the weather is so bad that parents should come to pick up their children, but it is quite rare for schools to close due to the weather, as Icelanders know how to get on with life even when there's lots of snow and heavy winds. We must admit that sometimes we smile when we see news of big cities overseas grinding to a halt due to levels of snowfall that are considered a normal day for us!

Until the age of 10, children can be enrolled in after-school care. After that, it is expected that kids look after themselves from the time school is out until their parents arrive home. Extended family members, grandparents in particular, often take an active role in the upbringing of children. The fact remains however that many children take care of themselves for a few hours each day from around the age of eight or nine.

Icelandic society is generally very safe and, as it's likely that both parents will work, children take responsibility for their own social lives. Icelandic parents don't organise play dates. Children will take their bikes or scooters and spend all day outside in summer, biking down to the beach or playing in wooded areas or parks, stealing rhubarb from gardens or jumping on trampolines.

One important feature of Icelandic society is the role of sports clubs. All neighbourhoods and towns have a local club that offers different types of sport to all ages. It's a given that the clubs will offer football and handball, along with other sports such as swimming, athletics, basketball, volleyball, tennis,

badminton, table tennis, karate or skiing. The clubs will go all the way to the premier league and enjoy strong support in their neighbourhoods. Sports coaches for all ages are professionally trained and the clubs have excellent facilities. This has been the secret of Iceland's success in international sport, particularly in men's and women's football and handball. Many kids also attend music school, dance or drama classes. Often these activities are organised locally, so kids attend them with their friends after school, without parental supervision. As a result of all this freedom, Icelandic children become quite independent at an early age, deciding for themselves how they spend their day after school ends at around two o'clock in the afternoon.

Parents usually use messaging apps to text each other, trying to locate their kids if they are still out when it is time to have dinner or, in a more traditional manner, stand at the door and shout '*matur!*' ('dinner!'). As it doesn't get dark at night during the summer, kids can go back out to play once they've eaten. It's not unusual to see children up to the age of 12 outside until 10 p.m. or even longer, while teenagers up to 16 can stay out until midnight as per police regulations.

Confirmation – Coming of Age

A confirmation ceremony affirms a child's baptism and their will to belong to the Christian faith, but it is traditionally considered as the passing from childhood to adulthood. As such, it is a very important turning point in the lives of Icelandic teenagers. In 2020, about 63 per cent of the population belonged to the Evangelical Lutheran Church of Iceland (the official Christian church) and most people will have been confirmed. Interestingly, confirmation as a symbolic coming-of-age ceremony is considered so important in Iceland that Siðmennt, the Icelandic Ethical Humanist Association, offers a secular alternative to non-religious children. While only a tiny minority of 13–14 year-olds had a 'civil confirmation' when it was first offered in 1989, that had risen to 13 per cent of all teenagers having a ceremony in 2020.

Confirmation season is normally around Easter; leading up to the event, children go to classes about religious matters at their church and attend mass in preparation. For the secular alternative, there is a course focused on themes such as critical thinking, ethics and human rights.

The confirmation is usually the first formal life event that a child will remember, having been too young to be aware of their baptism or naming ceremony. As such, confirmations are large celebrations, with extended family and friends of the parents usually in attendance. The young people being confirmed reap the rewards, as they tend to receive many gifts such as expensive tech gear, jewellery, books, camping equipment and money.

It's a Date

Dating is a relatively new phenomenon in Iceland and something Icelanders have perhaps picked up from Hollywood, but we are slowly learning how to do it. Traditionally, many Icelandic couples probably got to know each other through school, work or a hobby, such as a choir, sports, or via mutual friends. Others may have stumbled upon each other (literally) at a party or pub, or during a camping trip to one of the summer festivals.

With the arrival of apps and social media helping single people to find each other, Icelanders are beginning to go on actual dates. Going for coffee or a drink, having a walk or an *ísbíltúr* (see page 110), is often the first point of contact. However, Icelandic society is small, so you are quite likely to run into someone you know while on your first date. It can be especially awkward if you meet someone you *both* know and have to explain why the two of you are in each other's company.

Icelanders are fairly egalitarian, so women can feel comfortable indicating their interest in someone just as much as men can. It is sometimes said that Icelanders have a more casual view of sex than other countries and it is perhaps true that casual sex is less of a taboo.

This small society can, of course, create peculiar situations. You might find that someone you've started dating has already dated some of your friends and acquaintances in the past or might even have children with one of your childhood friends. Hence, we need words such as *kviðmágur* and *kviðsystir* (see page 78), although they are mostly used as a joke. Indeed, you may discover you share the same great-great grandparents, that your kids go to the same class at school, or that your mothers are good friends. While this can perhaps be awkward, there are also benefits – for example, it is easy to find out if someone you've just met is going to be a nightmare to deal with.

Put a Ring on It (or Not!)

If you ever find yourself at an Icelandic wedding, you'll probably see a happy couple in their thirties who have been together for a decade, surrounded by their children in the roles of ring-bearers and flower girls. The ceremony and reception will be relaxed and rather low-key, with the newlyweds paying for the whole thing themselves. If a bride has a large diamond ring, she has most likely bought it herself. There will be no wedding list, as the couple is likely to be on their second apartment and already have everything they need.

The Icelandic model for starting a family is quite unique. A couple will meet and fall in love, pregnancy follows and they decide to register as a cohabiting partnership. The first child is born, then a second (and sometimes more). Only then will the couple consider marriage, often largely for practical reasons. Registered cohabitation gives most of the same rights as marriage, apart from full legal protection in the case of separation or death. Many couples decide to skip marriage entirely.

In Iceland, there is absolutely no stigma attached to having a child outside of marriage – in fact, more than 70 per cent of children in Iceland are born to unmarried parents. The roots of this can be traced back to the nineteenth century, when people in debt or who didn't own land were not allowed to marry. Children born to cohabiting parents, while not a preferred choice, became a socially accepted fact. In modern-day Iceland, attitudes towards

starting a family can be explained by the relative freedom and financial independence of women (see page 54), as well as strong social protection policies and the close-knit extended-family support structure.

However, it would be incorrect to say that marriage is somehow an endangered social institution in Iceland, as most people do get married eventually and it is extremely easy to do so. You can marry within every religion (or no religion), including the neopagan Ásatrú. And, of course, same-sex marriages are legal.

Most Icelandic wedding ceremonies are surprisingly traditional, given the route couples take to get there. Most couples marry in a church and it is common for the mothers of the bride and groom to welcome the guests at the entrance, while the groom and his father are at the altar to greet everyone entering with a curt bow. The bride, even as she enters with her three children, will invariably be dressed in white.

Almost 40 per cent of marriages in Iceland end in divorce, but this is a relatively low figure compared to the rest of Europe. Perhaps there's something to be said about spending years together as parents before even considering tying the knot.

The (Blended) Icelandic Family

Given Icelanders' relaxed attitude to children and marriage, it is not surprising that family structures tend to be unconventional. In 2020, single-parent or cohabiting households with children slightly outnumbered traditional nuclear-family households. Blended families, where couples settle together with children from previous relationships, are also extremely common. With parents usually sharing custody rights and children often dividing their time equally between the two, many children grow up navigating a complex web of family relationships. For parents, logistics are often the greatest headache – ensuring that the children all have a place to themselves in their different homes, coordinating their after-school activities with their ex-partners, and the most complex puzzle of all: where everyone will spend Christmas Eve.

I Work, Therefore I Am

We have described the strong Icelandic work ethic in other chapters, so it should not come as a surprise that Icelanders retire later than most of their European counterparts. The official retirement age is 67, with most public-sector employees retiring at 70. Despite the relatively high retirement age – and in contrast to most countries, where people tend to stop working even before reaching it – Icelanders often remain active in the labour force well beyond the point they can stop.

Interestingly, the discourse around retirement in Iceland is not focused on how unfair it is that given the retirement age and life expectancy, the average Icelandic woman will only receive a pension for 18 years, while, for example, the average Dutch woman enjoys 23 years. Instead, the prominent National Association of Senior Citizens lobbies for more job opportunities for older people and for public-sector workers to be allowed to work for longer.

It isn't all work and no play for Icelandic pensioners, though. The country has been named the best place in the world to retire due to the good health, high life expectancy and general quality of life that pensioners enjoy. The diary of a typical fit and healthy 70 year old is likely to be busier than that of their children or even grandchildren, filled with travel, choir, Spanish lessons and seniors' Zumba.

Gone but Not Forgotten

If you have somehow made it through life in Iceland without publishing a book or becoming a public personality, rest assured that you will have your fifteen minutes of fame when you depart. In Iceland, the vast majority of people have their obituaries published in a newspaper and anyone can write them. Nowhere else in the world is the obituary so egalitarian. On the day of the funeral, newspapers will print (or publish online) obituaries about the deceased that are written by friends, family (even young children) and colleagues, often in the form of a personal letter to their loved one. If there isn't enough space in the newspaper, any remaining obituaries will appear in the next day's publication instead. Newspapers publish obituaries for free, partially as a public service, but also because they are extremely popular with readerships. Some people even admit that they subscribe to the national newspaper *Morgunblaðið* solely for its obituaries section.

The public nature of paying respects to the dead in the papers is also reflected in the size of Icelandic funerals, which are often announced on the radio and usually open to all. The funeral of someone with a large family and many friends can easily be attended by hundreds of people. There will be singing and live music, and everyone will be invited for coffee and cake afterwards.

Icelandic cemeteries are also surprisingly lively places, with graves tended by relatives for decades after a passing. They are often the site of family gatherings and remembrance, especially around birthdays and Christmas (see page 202).

The Icelandic approach to celebrating and remembering the dead is summed up in the following verse (often quoted in obituaries). It comes from the poem *Hávamál*, which was recorded in the thirteenth-century *Poetic Edda*, but is likely to have been written much earlier.

Deyr fé,
deyja frændur,
deyr sjálfur ið sama.
En orðstír
deyr aldregi
hveim er sér góðan getur.

Cattle die,
kindred die,
we ourselves also die;
but the fair fame
never dies
of him who has earned it.

HOLIDAYS AND CELEBRATIONS

Light in the Darkness – A Very Icelandic Advent

Given the short days and long winter nights in the far north, it is perhaps not surprising that Icelanders *love* to celebrate Christmas. People hang up lots of lights of all colours outside and inside of their houses (yes, a lot), attend Christmas concerts, throw parties, enjoy buffets, bake cookies and shop as if there were no tomorrow.

Celebrating *jól* (the same word as the English 'Yule') is an ancient tradition that dates back long before the arrival of Christianity. *Jól* was traditionally a midwinter solstice festival celebrated at the darkest time of year, either in December or January.

Aðventa, or Advent, marks the start of the Christmas season. Many people make or buy wreaths with four candles, lighting one candle on each of the Sundays leading up to Christmas until the last Sunday before, when all four candles are lit. Candles marking the 24 days of December before Christmas are also popular, where you burn one number off every day, while children also get Advent calendars with chocolate. Christmas preparations are taken seriously. Some think, for instance, that starting to decorate or play Christmas music before Advent should not be allowed. A common question in the run-up to Christmas is, 'Have you done everything?' What 'everything' entails is probably changing a bit these days, as younger generations are unlikely to clean every nook and cranny of their homes as their foremothers would have done during Advent (back then, housekeeping was a female job), preferring to focus more on enjoying the festive time with their families.

Almost all Icelandic homes own an *aðventuljós* (Advent light), which is put up at the start of the season. It is an inverted V-shape with seven candles, which might make visitors think of the Jewish menorah. There is no direct connection, though. There are seven lights solely because an uneven number is needed for the shape – you can sometimes get smaller ones with five or three lights. Having an *aðventuljós* was very popular in the 1960s and 70s, and is now considered an Advent essential. Hanging Advent stars or wreaths in windows is also common.

A *jólahlaðborð* is a Christmas buffet served in restaurants and hotels and is a big part of the festivities. Dishes on offer include traditional Icelandic foods as well as other local delicacies such as pickled herring with rye bread, pâtés, reindeer, ptarmigan, goose and duck, as well as marinated and smoked salmon, red cabbage, beetroot salads – the lot.

Decorating the tree was traditionally done on the day before Christmas Eve, but many have started to put theirs up earlier in December. Decorations often have an interesting history – they might have been inherited, made by a family member, are a gift from a previous Christmas, or have been bought during a particular holiday. The tree is either purchased from a florist or from various charities; alternatively, people can visit their local forest association and buy a tree which they can chop down themselves. The tradition of having a Christmas tree came to Iceland from Denmark in the late nineteenth century. As Iceland did not have much in the way of forests back then, a 'tree' was often made with wooden sticks and decorated with branches and candles, with little gifts hung on it.

The Yule Lads

Icelandic children are quite privileged when it comes to Christmas, but only if they behave themselves. Just one Santa Claus spreading joy and bringing presents isn't enough for kids in Iceland – there's a bunch of *jólasveinar*, or Yule lads, who each reward children in the run up to Christmas. Children put a shoe on their windowsill on the evening of 11 December, and if they have been good they will receive a small present in it each morning for the next 13 days. If they have been naughty, they are likely to get a potato – perhaps even a rotten one.

The Yule lads have a background of criminality that they have now left behind, but they still find it difficult to resist temptation, particularly when it comes to food or mischief. The lads live in a cave in the mountains with their ill-tempered troll parents, Grýla and Leppalúði. They are all many centuries old but are all still single, and that is not likely to change. Grýla, the mother, used to eat badly behaved children, but the story goes that she died of starvation some centuries ago, so Icelandic children no longer fear ending up in her pot.

The *jólasveinar* first appeared in written texts in the seventeenth century but their origins are likely to be much older. They are first described as horrible and dangerous trolls, but have slowly learned better manners, and towards the end of the nineteenth century they moved on from eating children themselves to the more moderate pursuits of stealing and pranks. These days, they now seem to have even given up on those, and have been giving shoe-presents since the 1960s. There is some confusion as to what they wear – sometimes they sport old-fashioned woollen clothes, but can also be spotted wearing red and white like Santa Claus, along with long white beards.

The most popular Yule lad of the lot is Stúfur, or 'Stubby'. He probably gained his popularity by the fact that he is the smallest of the brothers. Another of the most popular lads is Kertasníkir ('Candle-Stealer'), who is the last lad to arrive and therefore often brings the biggest present of the lot. Candles may have sometimes disappeared during the night of his visit, too. Many of the Yule lads like food. The first to arrive, Stekkjarstaur ('Sheepcote Clod'), tries to drink sheep milk straight from the udder, while Giljagaur ('Gully Gawk') prefers the milk froth. Þvörusleikir ('Spoon-Licker') likes the leftovers from unwashed spoons in the kitchen, while Pottaskefill ('Pot-Scraper') and Askasleikir ('Bowl Licker') also like to lick clean kitchen utensils. Then there is Skyrgámur ('*Skyr*-Gobbler'), who eats up all the delicious *skyr* in the home (who can blame him?). Bjúgnakrækir ('Sausage-Swiper') steals all the bangers he can lay his hands on, while Ketkrókur ('Meat-Hook') steals meat hanging from the rafters using a specially designed hook. Unfortunately for him, not many people hang their meat from the rafters these days. Then there is Gáttaþefur ('Doorway-Sniffer'), Gluggagægir ('Window-Peeper') and Hurðaskellir ('Door-Slammer'), all equally as mischievous. The total number of Yule lads is unknown, some Christmas songs describe a total of nine, and the aforementioned 13 are the ones who give children their presents. However, about 80 names have been found in records, some of them female.

Another key part of this Icelandic Christmas folklore is the Yulelads' family pet, *Jólakötturinn*, the Christmas Cat. It's a big, bloodthirsty feline that chases after children who haven't received any new clothes for Christmas and eats them alive. Isn't it festive?

Jólabakstur – The Great Icelandic Christmas Bake-Off

Baking *jólasmákökur* (Christmas cookies) is an absolute necessity during the festive season, and many families gather to prepare treats, with everyone providing a helping hand. The cookies get put into tins and during the holiday season people enjoy them at coffee time, or pretty much whenever they fancy something sweet. Previous generations used to make several types of cookies and households would sometimes compare how many varieties they had baked. With changing times, the number of types might have gone down – and some might even buy readymade dough to make life easier – but enthusiasm is still high.

Baking at Christmas became quite common in the 1920s. Before then, flour and sugar were hard to get, and it was even rare for people to have an oven. There are several varieties of cookies, with many of the recipes originating from Denmark. Among the most common are vanilla rings, gingerbread, chocolate-chip and *hálfmánar*, or 'half-moons'. To make *hálfmánar*, you roll out the dough then use a drinking glass to cut out rounds, put a dash of rhubarb or prune jam on one half of the round, then fold over the other side to create a half-moon. You then seal the edge with a fork, creating a line pattern as you go. There are also: *loftkökur*, or 'air cakes', which are superlight and similar to a chocolate meringue; *spesíur*, which are butter cookies decorated with a dab of chocolate; and other delights such as 'mother's kisses' and 'farmer cookies'. An absolute must in many households are 'Sarah Bernhardts'. Named after the French actress, these are almond macaroon cookies with a delicious silky filling made from cocoa, coffee, butter, egg yolks and salt, and dipped in dark chocolate. They have no historical link to Iceland, except that we absolutely love them. Last, but certainly not least, there is the *jólakaka*. The Icelandic Christmas cake is the only seasonal goodie that is actually named after Christmas, but is eaten all year round. It is a rather dry loaf cake with plenty of raisins and seasoned with cardamom – the perfect thing to have with coffee.

Laufabrauð

Another family activity centred around food is the cutting of the traditional *laufabrauð*, which translates literally as 'leaf bread'. *Laufabrauð* is a very thin, round flatbread. It's often said that the dough should be so thin that it is possible to read a newspaper through it. After flattening the dough and creating the round shape, each bread is decorated with leaf-like, geometric patterns, either cut by hand or created using a purpose-made brass roller. Each *laufabrauð* is then thrown into boiling oil or lard by the most experienced adult present, as this is the dangerous part of the endeavour. After being removed from the oil, the bread is flattened using a heavy pot or a specially made lid, which ensures that each *laufabrauð* is flat and allows the decorations to be enjoyed and admired before they are eaten. *Laufabrauð* is an excellent accompaniment for cured meat such as smoked lamb. They are even sometimes hung in windows as Christmas decorations. The original idea behind the recipe was to make as much bread as possible with the least amount of flour, as that was a rare, imported luxury. In addition, the deep-frying means *laufabrauð* can be stored for a long period of time.

The tradition of decorated, thin deep-fried bread is a purely Icelandic one that dates back centuries. At the time of writing, the Icelandic government is preparing to nominate the making of *laufabrauð* to UNESCO's Intangible Cultural Heritage of Humanity list.

Rotten Fish – An Icelandic Festive Favourite

It might seem like an odd thing to willingly allow the ammonic aroma of *kæst skata* (fermented skate) to permeate one's home at Christmas – yet this is something that many Icelandic households are happy to do. While many people do go to restaurants for their Christmas dose of rotten flat-fish to avoid the smell penetrating the home, and others prefer to cook it in the garden or garage, the fact remains that this is one Yuletide custom that is still popular.

This ancient practice comes from the Westfjords, the area close to where much of Iceland's skate is caught at this time of year, and has spread throughout the country. People were supposed to eat bad fish on 23 December, the day of Saint Þorlákur (Iceland's patron saint). It was all about fasting before Christmas and also to make the distinction greater with the Yuletide food to come. Over the centuries, people found ways to make fermented skate more appealing, and some people think of it as a delicacy. Others don't consider it food at all. The flavour is quite unique, but it could perhaps be likened to a cheese that is so strong that it brings tears to your eyes and melts the mucous membrane in your mouth!

The fermentation process is apparently quite simple. The wings of the skate are cut off and put into containers to rot. Skates don't have organs to pass urine, so it goes through the tissue and into the sea by osmosis. During the fermentation process, the flesh breaks down, releasing the ammonia and trimethylamine that cause both the specific smell and the taste. After around three weeks (depending on the temperature), the skate is considered to be ready. It is then boiled and served with potatoes and melted butter. Yum!

Gleðileg Jól (Merry Christmas)

Jól is seen as an important time to spend with family and friends, enjoying good food and company in a cosy atmosphere. No one is forgotten, either. The last part of the preparations (before taking a shower and putting the final touches to the Christmas dinner) is often to visit the cemetery to light candles for loved ones who have passed and put decorations on their graves.

Christmas is celebrated on the evening of Christmas Eve, starting officially at 6 p.m. RÚV, Iceland's national radio service, broadcasts the ringing of the church bells from Dómkirkjan, the cathedral in Reykjavík. These days, regardless of whether people are religious or not, it is quite common in Iceland to attend Christmas mass. After the radio presenter utters the words '*Gleðileg jól*' – 'Merry Christmas' – families embrace and also wish each other '*Gleðileg jól*'.

Many sit down to eat at the same time, and what is on the menu varies. While the national dish of lamb was usually the main option in the past, today

it can be substituted for meats such as ptarmigan, turkey, goose, reindeer or some other game. There are, of course, meat-free alternatives as well. Food is served with caramelised potatoes, red cabbage, pickled beetroot, and more. Dessert also varies, but an almond is always added to whatever it is, and the lucky person who finds it receives the *möndlugjöf*, or 'almond present'. This tends to be a gift that everyone can enjoy, such as a Christmas ornament or a jigsaw. Many people enjoy homemade ice cream for dessert, sometimes served with canned pear and its juice. Alternatively, there's *ris à l'amande*, a rice pudding with added whipped cream, almonds and cherries. In addition, some may prefer a trifle, a chocolate pudding, or even a *crème brûlée* or a *panna cotta*. Of course, an extravagant and delicious *hnallþóra* (see page 112) might appear. After dinner, some families dance around their Christmas tree and sing songs, before moving on to the presents.

Exchanging Christmas gifts is a rather new tradition in Iceland – it began in the late nineteenth century when children started to be given candles at Christmas. How Christmas presents are opened can vary. In many families, the tag on each present is read aloud (often by a child), then everyone watches each present being opened and even tried on if it's wearable (given that everyone wants to avoid a visit from the Christmas Cat, such gifts are vital), before turning to the next one. This can take quite a long time! In many families it is considered essential that each person is given a book, and many spend Christmas night reading it (see page 73).

Christmas Day tends to be when people meet extended family. Many families have *hangikjöt* (smoked lamb) with potatoes, beans and *laufabrauð* or *flatkökur* (rye flatbread), along with a Christmas ale. The day can be spent in pyjamas, while one continues to read their new books.

New Year's Eve to Twelfth Night

Mythical Creatures on the Move

According to folklore, elves move home on 31 December, leaving the rock or hill they have inhabited to find greener pastures elsewhere. Some people still follow a ritual of saying goodbye to elves who might be leaving, or welcoming elves who might be settling on their land or close by. It is important to have the elves on your side! If you want to try this, walk around your home on 31 December and say, 'Leave those who want to leave, come those who want to come, as long as no harm is done to my people and I'.

The Yule lads also start to leave, one by one, from Christmas Day onwards. By Þrettándinn, or Twelfth Night, on 6 January, the last Yule lad will have gone back to Grýla's cave and Christmas is officially over. Then decorations are taken down and some people attend a bonfire where the elves sometimes turn up as well. You might also see some leftover fireworks from New Year's Eve lighting up the sky.

Lighting Up the Sky

Áramót (literally, 'the juncture of years') is Iceland's New Year's Eve, and a unique experience that you really should have on your bucket list if you like fireworks, bonfires and parties.

At midnight, the skies are filled with fireworks going off everywhere you look. Almost every household will have their own display. When all this comes together, the result is the most magnificent display imaginable. It is perhaps not as glamorous as the displays right by the Eiffel Tower or the Sydney Harbour Bridge, but the fact that it is going on all around you and that you are taking part in creating this special show is the thrill. Every Icelander knows how to light fireworks and young children are given sparklers or even flaming torches (along with protective goggles).

Most people buy their fireworks from local rescue teams, who finance the bulk of their activities from the proceeds of such sales. As the rescue teams play a very important part in keeping the nation safe (see page 126), people see it as their obligation to buy lots of fireworks to support them.

In recent years, some Icelanders have started to question this tradition, not least for environmental reasons. It is possible to support the rescue teams by

donating a sum of money for them to plant trees to balance the greenhouse gas emissions produced by the fireworks. The loud explosions are also not always appreciated by pet owners and parents of young children!

Before the fireworks, Icelanders normally join their immediate family for dinner – with three to four generations all together, followed by visiting a bonfire to sing a few songs (often about elves) and perhaps even light a few early rockets. After that, we get ready to watch *Áramótaskaupið*, the annual TV show that mocks the year now coming to an end. This is something that almost the entire population sits down to watch, and the talk by the coffee machine at work over the next few days will be all about it. During the show, the fireworks usually come to almost a complete stop. However, after the programme finishes, the explosions start again with greater vigour than before. At midnight, the fireworks come to a culmination, with the sky lit up in different colours and shapes. Later on, the young make their way to clubs or parties organised by friends. Downtown Reykjavík on New Year's Eve is great fun. The square in front of Hallgrímskirkja church is a superb spot to be at midnight, as you have a great view over the city. Never go to bed just after midnight, as the party is only just starting.

Midwinter Celebrations

Husband's Day and *Þorrablót*

Bóndadagur, or 'Husband's Day', takes place on the first day of the old Icelandic month Þorri, which arrives towards the end of January and marks the exact middle of winter. It is a day when men are given extra-special treats from their partners or lovers – it could be described as an Icelandic version of Valentine's Day, but for men only. According to an old tradition, the man of the house is supposed to welcome Þorri by getting up early, taking off his shirt and jumping around the outside of the home on one leg, with one leg in his trousers and the other trouser leg dragging behind him.

Þorri is also the month when Icelanders gather for the great midwinter party known as Þorrablót to eat traditional foods such as preserved ram's testicle and shark, along with singed and boiled sheep's head (see page 102). Many Icelandic men will receive a platter of these meats with their favourite bottle of locally brewed beer or a bottle of Brennivín (see page 114) from their partners. Nothing says 'I love you' quite like a fermented ram's testicle.

Woman's Day

Of course, there is also a day to celebrate women. This is *Konudagur*, or 'Woman's Day', falling on the first Sunday of the old Icelandic month *Góa*, which comes after Þorri in late February.

Traditionally, families would enjoy a good meal on *Konudagur*, but in the early twentieth century, shops started to advertise gifts to give on the day. Today, many women receive flowers, a box of chocolates or even jewellery from their partners. The winning cake in the annual 'Cake of the year' competition of the National Association of Bakers is sold in bakeries around the country on *Konudagur*, so that is the perfect gift for women with a sweet tooth!

As you can imagine, with Husband's Day and Woman's Day, there is no real need for Valentine's Day in Iceland. Especially as Woman's Day falls only a few days after 14 February, when Valentine's Day is celebrated.

Bun Day to Easter

Bun Day

If chocolate buns are your thing, then *Bolludagur* ('Bun Day') is for you. It always falls on the day before Shrove Tuesday, seven weeks before Easter. In the morning, children wake their parents by playfully smacking them on the bottom with a purpose-made stick they have decorated at school, and shouting '*bolla!*' ('bun!'). They are then entitled to consume as many buns as the number of times they manage to scream the word before their parents get out of bed. If they manage to say '*bolla, bolla, bolla*', they receive three buns.

The bun is made with choux pastry and is filled with whipped cream, often with a dab of jam, and topped with chocolate icing. Bakeries are very busy on Bolludagur and you can get lots of different icings and cream fillings such as caramel, Baileys, strawberry, Nutella and, of course, liquorice (see page 108).

How To Do *Bolludagur* at Home

It is quite acceptable to eat buns for breakfast on *Bolludagur*, but make sure you have enough to last throughout the day, because you'll want some for dessert after lunch. And with coffee in the afternoon. And as dessert after dinner. And why not have one before bed? After all, it's 'explosion day' tomorrow (see page 210), so better get your stomach used to it!

Ingredients
For the choux pastry:
100 g (3½ oz) butter
200 ml (⅓ pint) water
1 tsp sugar
100 g (3½ oz) plain (all-purpose) flour
3 eggs

For the filling:
Whipped cream, jam, or anything you like!

For the icing:
160 g (5½ oz) icing (confectioners') sugar
2 tbsp cocoa powder (unsweetened)
2 tsp vanilla essence (extract)
2 tbsp brewed coffee
3 tbsp water

Makes around 20 buns.

In a pan, bring the butter, water and sugar to a boil. Remove from the heat and gradually mix in the flour until you have a soft dough that can be easily removed from the pan or the wooden spoon.

Place the dough in a bowl and leave to cool for 15 minutes. Meanwhile, preheat the oven to 240°C/220°C Fan (425°F/Gas Mark 7). Mix in the eggs, one at a time, until you have a firmer but pliable, enhanced dough (you can use an electric mixer if you wish).

Use two teaspoons to dollop equal amounts of dough onto a lined baking tray, leaving plenty of space between each one. You should be able to fill two regular-sized baking trays with 9-10 buns on each.

Bake each tray separately on the bottom shelf for about 20–25 minutes, or until golden. Don't open the oven until the very end.

Remove from the oven and leave them to cool on a wire rack. Slice open each bun horizontally, stopping just before you slice all the way through. Fill each bun with whipped cream and rhubarb jam – an Icelandic favourite – or whatever else you might like, just use your imagination!

To make the icing, mix all the ingredients together using a whisk and spread generously on the buns.

Explosion Day

Iceland's Shrove Tuesday is known as *Sprengidagur* – 'Explosion Day'. As if the previous day's gorging on buns wasn't quite enough, the following day brings a hefty portion of salted lamb and split-pea soup (*saltkjöt og baunir*). Many people say you are supposed to eat so much that your stomach feels like it is going to explode – hence the name. There is another explanation for the name, as the similar German word *Sprengtag*, referring to the sprinkling of holy water, may be a more religious explanation for the start of Lent.

Ash Wednesday

Öskudagur, or Ash Wednesday, traditionally marks the start of fasting during Lent. Children celebrate by dressing up in costumes and singing to shop keepers in exchange for sweets. Sometimes there is a large container of sweets that children take turns in hitting with a stick until all the goodies fall out, which is referred to as 'hitting the cat out of the barrel'. An additional, but disappearing, custom is for people to make little cloth bags, sometimes fill them with ash, then attach them to the backs of innocent passers-by without them realising.

Easter

Icelanders get three days off work at *Páskar* (Easter), so many use the weekend to travel, either at home or abroad. If Easter comes early in the year, skiing conditions are often quite good. Many also go to their summer houses. Maundy Thursday, the day of the Last Supper, is called *Skírdagur* and is the first day of the holiday. *Föstudagurinn langi*, or Good Friday, used to be taken very seriously. It was absolutely forbidden to have any kind of fun, as it was considered disrespectful to Christ and his suffering. Children were not allowed to play any games in the olden days, and many children thought the name of the day, which literally translates as 'Long Friday', had to do with time passing extremely slowly. These days, children laugh and play games, but shops are closed all day, while bars and pubs only open on the stroke of midnight.

Páskadagur (Easter Sunday) is often celebrated with a family lunch of lamb, accompanied by caramelised potatoes, peas and red cabbage. With so much chocolate eaten on this day, there isn't really any need for a specific dessert. Easter-egg hunts take place indoors, with the egg hidden somewhere slightly visible, such as behind books in a bookcase or in a leafy plant.

The eggs are made by local chocolatiers. They vary in size but will have either a little decorative chick or other figurine on top. They'll also be filled with sweets (lots of liquorice, naturally) and, most importantly, there will be a written proverb hidden inside. Sayings such as 'wise men can have stupid descendants' could perhaps cause a bit of a stir at a family party, but normally they are something more neutral, such as 'everyone is the creator of their own fortune'. Some, like 'one bite won't hurt', might even help you to eat your chocolate egg without guilt.

The First Day of 'Summer'

If you ever see a windswept marching band parading through the streets of any Icelandic town on a Thursday towards the end of April, then you have probably stumbled across celebrations for the official arrival of summer.

The first day of summer is really the most Icelandic holiday there is, and is very dear to us Icelanders – not just because it is a day off work or school. Children are given presents, usually something to use during the warmer days ahead, such as sports gear, skipping ropes or other toys to use outdoors. This is a very old tradition, dating back to the early sixteenth century, much older than giving Christmas presents. Parades are organised in the different neighbourhoods and there are often barbecued hotdogs afterwards, or ice cream (of course).

The celebration of the first day of summer goes back centuries. In fact, there are only two seasons – summer and winter – in the traditional Icelandic calendar, which dates back to the twelfth century. The first day of summer falls on the first Thursday after 18 April. In contrast, the first day of winter, towards the end of October, is no longer celebrated. In the first centuries following the colonisation of Iceland, the day was a pagan event.

You might find it peculiar that summer's arrival is in April, when it can still be very cold. The average temperature at this time of year is only around 2–3°C (35–37°F), and sometimes it even snows on the first day of summer. Indeed, the weather means that the marching bands can sometimes struggle to read

their music or have to stop it flying away with the wind altogether (which might be why they are known as wind bands!). However, for Icelanders, there is no such thing as bad weather, just bad clothing, so people will happily wear woolly hats and winter mittens for the summer parade.

Other milestones also herald the arrival of summer. People who live in the narrow fjords of the far north-west, surrounded by tall mountains, don't see the sun from late November until late January. When it finally rises above the mountains, allowing the rays to reach down to the bottom of the fjords, locals celebrate with coffee and pancake parties.

The most important sign that summer is on the way is the arrival of the *lóa*. The bird, known as the golden plover in English, is a migrant that spends its winters on the European continent and comes to Iceland in the spring to lay its eggs on wind-barren heaths. The *lóa* usually arrives towards the end of March, and it is a major news story when the first one is spotted. A bird with a sweet melancholic song, the *lóa* is sometimes referred to as 'the sweet harbinger of spring' and no other bird is as beloved. A much-loved children's song about the bird starts with the line, 'The golden plover has arrived to bid farewell to the snow, to bid farewell to boredom, this she can do. She has told me that the whimbrel will come soon, sunshine in the valleys and flowers in the fields'.

Eurovision – Douze Points!

The Eurovision Song Contest is neither a tradition nor a holiday, but it is an event that Icelanders love to love (or love to hate). Every year, it is met with great enthusiasm. In 2016, a staggering 95.3 per cent of those watching television at the time were tuned in to the Eurovision final.

Iceland has, at the time of writing, never won Eurovision. However, it has come second twice in 1999 (*All Out Of Luck*, performed by Selma Björnsdóttir) and in 2009 (*Is It True?*, sung by Jóhanna Guðrún). Iceland was hotly tipped to be the winner in 2020, when Daði and his electro-pop band Gagnamagnið took the world by storm with their song *Think About Things*. Sadly, the contest was cancelled for the first time ever due to the COVID-19 pandemic, so we will never know if they would have won. However, the song was chosen by *Time* magazine as number six of the 10 best songs of 2020 and Daði was selected to compete again in 2021.

Eurovision is a party for the whole family. It is helpful that Iceland is two hours behind Central European Time when the competition takes place in spring, so the show starts at the child-friendly hour of 7 p.m. Many invite friends and family over, light up the barbecue and make cocktails. Kids absolutely love Eurovision and will, like the rest of the nation, support the Icelandic entry all the way – even when the act is a BDSM-inspired technoband called Hatari, or 'Hater' (2019).

Fishermen's Day

The important work of fishermen is celebrated in coastal towns and villages around the country on *Sjómannadagurinn* ('Fishermen's Day'), usually the first Sunday in June. Participants usually try their luck at activities such as swimming in the sea in full fishing gear, rowing, balancing on buoys while pillow-fighting, tugs of war, and so on. Retired fishermen will be given awards for their important contribution and politicians give speeches about the vital importance of fishing to Icelandic society.

The day was first marked in 1938 to remember fishermen lost at sea, but quickly became a festival. Legislation was passed in 1987 to ensure that fishermen and most other seafarers have this day off and will be on land so they can join the festivities, which often last for a few days.

Hæ, hó, jibbí, jei! – Icelandic National Day

Iceland declared independence from Denmark on 17 June 1944 at Þingvellir, the old site of the parliament. The day was chosen because it was the birthday of Jón Sigurðsson, the nineteenth-century leader of Iceland's struggle for self-rule. You'll find his picture on the 500-króna note and there's a statue of him in front of the parliament building in Reykjavík.

Þjóðhátíðardagurinn, Icelandic National Day, is celebrated all over the country on 17 June. Part of the official celebrations is the recital of a poem in front of Parliament by the *fjallkona* – the 'lady of the mountain' – who is a personification of Iceland as a woman. The *fjallkona* will often be an actress and she will recite a poem that has been written specifically for the occasion, which will be televised live. Smaller towns might also have their own *fjallkona*.

In the afternoon, Icelanders flock to the streets waving flags, with marching bands leading the way. Some might even dress in national costume.

Festival Weekend

The biggest weekend for travel in Iceland is the *Verslunarmannahelgi* ('traders' holiday'). The first Monday in August is a public holiday in Iceland, so Icelanders pack their camping gear and head to the countryside. This weekend is the main festival weekend of the year.

The biggest festival is held in Vestmannaeyjar (see page 16), the archipelago off the south coast. People camp in the valley and enjoy concerts. On the final night, there's a big bonfire with fireworks and everyone gathers for the *brekkusöngur* ('slope-singing'), sitting together on the hillside facing the main stage, singing well-known Icelandic songs while accompanied by a local celebrity on the guitar. The locals of Vestmannaeyjar have their own special area at the festival where they put up large white tents and even bring furniture to make them well-equipped! This is where they'll have their own party going on, playing the guitar and singing, eating local food and consuming lots of alcohol. Since 1901, the festival has only been cancelled three times – in 1914 (due to the outbreak of the First World War), in 1973 (due to a large volcanic eruption on the island), and in 2020 (due to COVID-19).

Reykjavík Pride

One of the biggest festivals in the capital area is Reykjavík Pride. It is a six-day festival in mid-August that celebrates LGBTQIA+ people, human rights, culture and diversity. Pride was first celebrated in Reykjavík in its current form in 1999 and is treated as a big party for everyone. There are concerts, drag shows, events dedicated to the history of LGBTQIA+ people in Iceland, and more – the programme varies from year to year. The festival culminates on the Saturday, when families go to watch the parade and wave rainbow flags. The parade features lots of decorated trucks representing different groups within the communities, such as queer families, the elderly, and the choir, as well as groups of friends who try to outdo each other's decorations and costumes. The most extravagant float usually belongs to Páll Óskar, one of Iceland's favourite singers and a former Eurovision contestant. Attitudes towards the LGBTQIA+ community have changed drastically in the last two decades and Iceland is considered as one of the most welcoming countries in the world.

Regional Festivals

There are various local festivals celebrated every year around the country, often highlighting the history of the area where they are held.

Vetrarhátíð: A winter festival held in Reykjavík in February to light up the darkest period of the year during the old month of Þorri.

Bíladagar: On the third weekend in June, Akureyri celebrates cars, with racing and 'drifting', where cars are intentionally oversteered to terrifying effect.

Humarhátíð á Höfn: A June festival dedicated to lobster in Höfn, the capital of this tasty crustacean.

Miðaldadagar á Gásum: This festival held in July each year in Gásir, an old Viking trading post and archaeological site close to Akureyri, showcases life in medieval Iceland, featuring different industries such as ironwork, pottery and weapon-making.

Írskir dagar á Akranesi: 'Irish days' are celebrated at the beginning of July every year in Akranes, commemorating Iceland's Celtic origins from the slaves brought by the first settlers, mainly from Ireland and Scotland. There is also a competition to find the most red-haired Icelander.

Franskir Dagar á Fáskrúðsfirði: Fáskrúðsfjörður's 'French days', also in July, remembers the time when French fishing boats were regular visitors (see page 17) – also reflected in the town's street signs, which are in both Icelandic and French.

Fiskidagurinn mikli: 'The Great Fish Day' in Dalvík is held on the second weekend of August. Local fish factories offer visitors a taste of lots of different delicacies, while locals invite guests into their homes to taste their famous fish soup.

Menningarnótt: Reykjavík Culture Night is held on the Saturday closest to 18 August, when Reykjavík was founded in 1786. In recent years, the current mayor and his family have invited everyone to drop by their home for waffles. It is the day of the Reykjavík Marathon and there are concerts, art exhibitions and performances, culminating in an outdoor concert and fireworks display.

Picture Credits

Front cover: © Jón Gunnar Árnason/Myndstef. Photography © Gunnar Freyr Gunnarsson, www.icelandicexplorer.com.
Inside: Photography © Gunnar Freyr Gunnarsson, www.icelandicexplorer.com, with the following exceptions:

173 all except tl, 174, 197, 202, 206: Nína Björk Jónsdóttir.

23bl Lucia Pitter/Shutterstock; 35tl Udo Bernhart/Alamy; 35br Charles Mahaux/Alamy; 43b Matthew Micah Wright/Getty; 49 Ingólfur Bjargmundsson/Getty; 52 Kieran Mcmanus/BPI/Shutterstock; 57 From the book *Vigdís – kona verður forseti*, by Páll Valsson, JPV, Iceland, 2009. Photographer unknown; 68 Viking World. Photo © Renata Marcolova; 72 copyright their respective publishers; 73 Arctic-Images/Getty; 82t Gonzales Photo – Per Lange/Alamy; 82cl Lorne Thomson/Redferns/Getty; 82cr Santiago Felipe/Getty; 82b Frank Hoensch/Redferns/Getty; 83tl Amy Harris/Invision/AP/Shutterstock; 83tr REUTERS/Mario Anzuoni/Alamy; 83cl Stefan Hoederath/Redferns/Getty; 83cr Shutterstock; 83b Mark Horton/Getty Images; 86 © Shoplifter. Image by Ugo Carmeni; 87l Ragnar Th Sigurðsson/Alamy; 87r Danuta Hyniewska/Alamy; 88 Henk Vrieselaar/Shutterstock; 89 copyright their respective studios; 90 Aurum by Guðbjörg, Sand collection. Photographer: David Abrahams, Stylist: Inga Harðardóttir.; 91l Farmer's Market. Photo: Ari Magg; 91r Reykjavik Raincoats. Photo by Magnús Andersen; 92tl Anna Thorunn. Photo: Anna Thorunn Hauksdottir; 92tc Lulla Doll by RoRo, photo by Gunnar Freyr Gunnarsson; 92tr Scintilla. Photo by Helena Manner and Annecy Dubrunfaut; 92bl IHANNA HOME. Photo by Karl Petersson; 92br Tulipop. Photo: Ragna M Guðmundsdóttir; 94l dpa/Alamy Live News; 94r Ragnar Th Sigurðsson/age fotostock/SuperStock; 95l Eistnaflug: Marketing East Iceland (CC BY 2.0). Photo by Stefanía Ósk Ómarsdóttir; 95r Ragnar Th Sigurðsson/Alamy; 99r Lindsay Snow/Shutterstock; 113 Photo by Hákon Davíð Björnsson, Chef: Folda Guðlaugsdóttir, Stylist: Hanna Ingibjörg Arnarsdóttir, Magazine: *Gestgjafinn*; 126, 127 www.sosfotos.com; 129l Vitalii Matokha/Shutterstock; 129r Cavan Images/Alamy; 130l Gareth McCormack/Alamy; 131l Maridav/Shutterstock; 131r Audunn Nielsson and the Arctic Open; 148tl, tr, bl Photographer: Hallur Karlsson, Magazine: *Hús og híbýli*; 148br Photographer: Hákon Davíð Björnsson, Magazine: *Hús og híbýli*; 153 Kristín Hrafnhildur Hayward; 159 Leikflokkur Húnaþings vestra. Photo by Hulda Signý Jóhannesdóttir; 161t nikolaskus/Shutterstock; 161b Improvisor/Shutterstock; 162 Karas Uiliia/Shutterstock; 180–81 Frosti Heimisson; 188–89 Arctic-Images/Getty; 190 Torbjörn Arvidson/Alamy; 203 Carolyne Parent/Shutterstock; 208 Brauð & Co, Reykjavik, Iceland; 212–13 Ryzhkov Sergey/Shutterstock; 214 Ulrich Perrey/dpa/Alamy; 218 Arctic-Images/Getty; 219 Jón Heiðar Ragnheiðarson – www.stuckiniceland.com; 221tl Fiskidagurinn mikli. Photo by HSH; 221tr kondr.konst/Shutterstock; 221c Fáskrúðsfjörður: Marketing East Iceland (CC BY 2.0); 221br Irish Days: Akraneskaupstaður municipality. Photo by Myndsmiðjan.

About the Authors

In the autumn of 1984, at the ages of 8 and 9, we both took our first steps into a new school, Hlíðaskóli in Reykjavík. We had both recently moved to a brand new neighbourhood, jokingly nicknamed *Milli lífs og dauða* ('Between life and death'), as it was situated between the city's hospital and the cemetery.

We immediately became best friends and were more or less attached at the hip through elementary school, high school and college. For as long as we can remember we've had a shared passion of writing. As children we worked as presenters on the children's radio show *Barnaútvarpið* at the National Radio, we wrote and performed plays on the radio and at school and even on the big stage in Reykjavík during Iceland's National Day celebrations in 1987. We aspired to become great actresses, which did not come to fruition!

We ended up following similar career paths, both working in the international arena. Edda for various international bodies as an expert in the field of global health. Nína as a diplomat, working for the Icelandic Foreign Service, after first starting a career in journalism. Nína was also a tourist guide for a few years and has travelled all over Iceland, both through work and with her rescue team.

Although Edda has mostly lived abroad since 1996, each time we meet it feels like we just met yesterday. Nína has spent a quarter of her life abroad, so we have both spent countless hours explaining the peculiarities of our beloved homeland to friends and colleagues from around the world. Nína lives in Reykjavík with her two children. Edda lives in Geneva, Switzerland with her husband and two children. We are godmothers to each other's firstborns.

In 2020, Nína wrote a children's book on Icelandic heroines throughout history, *Íslandsdætur* (*Daughters of Iceland*). This led to us writing the book you are now holding: *How to Live Icelandic*. We hope you have enjoyed reading it as much as we enjoyed writing it.

Love and thanks to our families for their support and help in delving into the Icelandic psyche, not to mention putting up with weeks of furious typing, loud late-night phone conversations and for always cheering us on, however crazy the project got.

Heartfelt thanks to our amazing group of friends for advice on everything from earthquakes to dairy farming, and for being so photogenic. Big thanks also to everyone at Quarto.

Brimming with creative inspiration, how-to projects and useful information to enrich your everyday life, Quarto Knows is a favourite destination for those pursuing their interests and passions. Visit our site and dig deeper with our books into your area of interest: Quarto Creates, Quarto Cooks, Quarto Homes, Quarto Lives, Quarto Drives, Quarto Explores, Quarto Gifts, or Quarto Kids.

First published in 2021 by White Lion Publishing,
an imprint of The Quarto Group.
The Old Brewery, 6 Blundell Street
London, N7 9BH,
United Kingdom
T (0)20 7700 6700
www.QuartoKnows.com

Text © 2021 Nína Björk Jónsdóttir and Edda Magnus
Photography © 2021 Gunnar Freyr Gunnarsson, www.icelandicexplorer.com, except where otherwise stated

Nína Björk Jónsdóttir and Edda Magnus have asserted their moral rights to be identified as the Authors of this Work in accordance with the Copyright Designs and Patents Act 1988.

All rights reserved. No part of this book may be reproduced or utilised in any form or by any means, electronic or mechanical, including photocopying, recording or by any information storage and retrieval system, without permission in writing from White Lion Publishing.

Every effort has been made to trace the copyright holders of material quoted in this book. If application is made in writing to the publisher, any omissions will be included in future editions.

A catalogue record for this book is available from the British Library.

ISBN 978-0-7112-6737-4
Ebook ISBN 978-0-7112-6739-8

10 9 8 7 6 5 4 3 2 1

Design by Ginny Zeal

Printed in China